# A STUDENT'S GUIDE TO *Intellectual* WORK

*BY* JEAN GUITTON

*Translated by*
ADRIENNE FOULKE

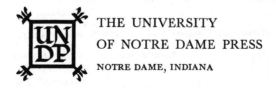

THE UNIVERSITY
OF NOTRE DAME PRESS
NOTRE DAME, INDIANA

*The original French title of this book is*
*LE TRAVAIL INTELLECTUEL*
*published in 1951 by*
*Aubier Editiones Montaigne, Paris*

*Printing History*
First Printing ........................ 1964
Second Printing .................... 1965

*Library of Congress Catalog Card Number: 64-22121*

*Manufactured in the United States*
*By North State Press, Inc.*
*Hammond, Ind.*

# Introduction

This little book has a similar purpose to that of its predecessor, my "New Art of Thinking." It is born of a deep friendliness I feel for students, especially for students who feel painfully confused or alone, and its aim is to help them in their work. Hopefully, it may free them of any sense of inferiority or strain.

At the same time, the book is addressed to people who are caught up in the hurly-burly of modern life but who have not, for all that, given up reading, writing, and thinking.

It is even addressed to people who are proficient in these things, for in matters of knowledge, style, and speech we are all apprentices, and, as Goethe used to say, it is good to learn to do the smallest thing in the largest way.

Observation bears out the fact that when you are young, a teacher rarely teaches you how to work. He gives you assignments, he judges and grades your papers; sometimes—this happens more frequently as you advance—he suggests that you correct and recopy a paper, or he shows you a model, perhaps one he has written himself, of how it should have been done. But he hardly ever tells you how he has gone about it; this part of your learning process he leaves to chance or to your own best inspiration. It is this lack of experience in *how to do* the thing that largely accounts for the fact that so many young people become discouraged about their studies.

For that matter, all of you, at every stage in your lives, fail to make full use of your mental energy. You have so much of it that it never occurs to you to be mindful of how you should use it! And yet if you applied yourselves better, you could with the same amount of effort accomplish so much more. It is scarcely thinkable how much more smoothly and fully you would live if you had greater skill and patience. Now, it is true that you cannot be told how to function; this is not communicable, and each must make his own mistakes. But I know, also, that I have been greatly helped by books that deal with methods of work, which fact has encouraged me to develop such ideas further by writing this book.

The reader must not expect any panaceas. I am reviving quite simple ideas that are present, I believe, in the oldest teaching traditions of my country. You will see that the mind must learn to concentrate and, whatever the subject matter may be, discover at what point to approach a problem; that it must make leisure as well as the mere passage of time contribute to its own maturing; that to know itself it must express itself, for form and substance cannot be separated (which is why we will talk later about style); and, finally, that there is no human state or condition in which it is impossible to think (and that is why we will talk about how the mind can work in periods of fatigue or trouble).

In writing this little manual, I have been guided by the way in which students work in an artist's studio.

The artist does not proceed like an instructor in literature or science. You watch him work. In turn, you try your hand at copying or sketching from a live model. Now and then you will hear him muttering at your shoulder. He tells you to move aside, and there before your eyes he corrects your sketch. To my mind, such methods are worth all the lecture courses in the world. I will go even further and say that I would rather spend one single day observing a novelist—J. F. Powers, for example—at work in his study than to attend courses for months on end.

This is why—like Descartes, who told his own life story before he began explaining his Method—I will relate some personal experiences through which I rediscovered the unchanging rules of the art of working. You, too, will have to learn from your experiences; otherwise all my advice will be quite useless.

Finally, I must say that the suggestions I will make here do not necessarily suit every mind and temperament. I have not tried to be all-inclusive but only to be useful to the people for whom this book is intended.

# Contents

INTRODUCTION                                    iii

1 WATCHING OTHER PEOPLE WORK                      1

2 PREPARATION OF WORK                            21

3 THE PROFOUND EFFORT                            35

4 THE MONSTER AND HIS REST                       47

5 PUTTING YOUR THOUGHTS IN ORDER                 61

6 READING AS SELF-ENRICHMENT                     77

7 SEEDS AND HUSKS                                91

8 NOTES AND COURSES                             105

9 WRITING AND STYLE                             121

10 WORKING WHILE TIRED OR SICK                  137

11 EXCERPTS FROM A LETTER TO A YOUNG MAN        151

# 1

# Watching Other
# People Work

To be dissatisfied when you are young with the way you are taught is both necessary and honorable. Flawless teaching would be ineffectual in forming a man; if the child is to attain his full adult stature, he needs to be treated adeptly—but ineptly, too. The vice of rigidly systematic education is that it can produce only a child-man, which happened to many young princes in the past and perhaps even to Jean Jacques Rousseau's Emile. So thank heaven that your early teachers have defects and inadequacies, for otherwise you would have nothing to react against. Conflict is an essential of first-hand experience. A teacher instructs you by what he gives you, yes, but he also stimulates you by his very deficiences; he pushes you on to becoming your own inner teacher.

Few of you have the leisure in your middle years to review the first stage of your life journey, to judge it from the perspective of maturity, and to set about re-learning the alphabet, as it were. When such taking stock of self is possible, there is an advantage in its being combined with some kind of privation. In our twentieth-century world many of you reach the famous fortieth milestone in life to find yourselves in circumstances far different from what you had expected—in a small town; in a foreign country, whether from choice or as exiles; in a political underground group; or even in jail. It is under such unforeseeable conditions that you experience this kind of second birth. I should like to relate what five years of confinement in a German prison camp taught me about the work of the mind.

In such circumstances, one of the first things to strike you is that you lack everything you had until then thought of as necessities; you are reduced to paying attention to what goes on around you, to memory, and to a very occasional conversation. This gradually brings you around to deciding that books are not indispensable, after all, or that very few suffice. Our civilization is so surfeited with information and with means of learning, it offers so many masks and false supports, that a man can no longer tell what he does or does not know. The proof that you know something, Aristotle said, is that you are able to teach it. In that prison period of no books or notes, I measured how little the most knowledgeable knew—yet that little, when it was pulled from their very insides, they taught well.

The first winter was spent without pen or ink. Paper was scarce. There was no quiet table, no calm corner, but a perpetual moving to and fro; it was like having to work in the kitchen, the way so many poor children must, surrounded by dirty dishes and forced to employ all their powers of concentration just to shut out the clatter. But little by little, with long periods of waiting in between, the tools of work were given back to us. I really believe that if pens, notebooks and books had been restored to us all at once, we would have been bowed down again under too much plenty.

Imprisonment puts the various kinds of culture that we acquire in school to a new kind of test. The men in our camp, anywhere from twenty to fifty years old, had been snatched up at the peak of their powers and forcibly presented with the one blessing men are forever seeking and almost never find—leisure. A whole day in which they had nothing to do, a day they could devote to learning, if they wanted to. Every nation is characterized by what its people most readily rebuild, when they must, from scratch: for the English it is a club; for the Poles it is an army, or the kernel of an army; for the Russians it is a community; for the Moslems, a place of prayer; and for the French what grew out of prison soil was a school, a university in embryo.

When you are young you work alone. With time life allows you to see others at work, too. Yet the person who is working does not like to be watched; he is probably right to hide behind an activity that reveals him so clearly and that he has learned with such effort. People who work with their hands are less shy, however, and it is a good thing, as Descartes pointed out, to watch the simplest kinds of work being performed and to see the ways in which they are related. Each of you is like a cyclone, and whether you suck up grains of sand or particles of gold does not matter; the image of breathing is the same. Chance or some conditioning circumstance makes you choose such and such profession, such and such way of doing things. Would it not be a good idea to see yourselves in a quite different aspect—for example, to ask yourselves, "If I were a potter, how would I set about it?" Or "If I were President, how would I handle the job?" By asking such questions, you preserve in yourselves the universal man; you keep your minds above the level of your own particular work—

indeed, of all work. You differ from one another much
less than you think you do. As draftees in the army, both
the farmer and lawyer are equally astonished that they
can learn and carry out new duties so easily. *The value
of your jobs, in other words, is determined by the spirit
and the inner order that you invest in them and in
yourselves as you carry them out.*

## II

Prior to my prison-camp days, I knew very little
about elementary schoolteachers. What unrecognized
greatness there is in this breed of humans, rooted in the
earth but flowering in the mind! Our grade teacher is
generally a newcomer to the kingdom of knowledge. He
is rather defensively proud, for he fears, especially when
assigned to teaching in a small town, that the clergyman
or banker, whose status has been so long established,
will snatch away the precious possession that he has only
newly acquired and that has set him free. But the schoolteacher, more than any other person, possesses the virtues of the land, applied, in his case, to the cultivation
of the intelligence. Learning for him is a labor that
cannot be pleasant in itself. Yet this kind of man set
himself a rigorous study program in camp. How few
people really learn a language as adults without going
abroad! To learn a language forces you to go through
rigid maneuvers—memorizing conjugations, writing out
exercises of graduated difficulty, and so forth, all of
which calls for no small amount of will power. Was it
easier for the schoolteachers in camp because their back-
ground had accustomed them to hard work? Was it
that, being used to disciplining children, they were wise
or proud enough to impose self-discipline on them-

selves? I never saw one of them work in an amateurish way; they set about a task in the same spirit of patient, slow-moving implacability with which the woodcutter confronts each new tree. The time clergy usually devote to religious services, and the deep feeling with which they conduct them, these teachers transferred to their intellectual work, which they clearly thought of as a holy office of intelligence. What they often lacked, on the other hand, was a kind of abandon, a relaxed turn of speech, a sereneness of will. Intellectual work demands of us two opposing attitudes: a struggle against distraction or dispersion of effort, which we can avoid only through concentration; and, at the same time, a detachment in relation to our work, since, as Etienne Pascal said, the mind must rise and be held above the level of its immediate task.

To our "clergy," whether lay or ecclesiastical, this second virtue often appears as laziness. Our schoolteachers are so passionately involved in learning whatever it is they want to learn that often they are possessed by what they know rather than possessing, and therefore being able to pass on, their knowledge. For the same reason, there is a curious difference between their natural and their educated selves. Leave them to their own good common sense and their personal experience, and they will think and express themselves very well. But they cherish the notion that science or philosophy calls for high-flown, obscure language. Every good editor can help an author to communicate by showing him how to express himself simply and forcefully.


III


Those of us in camp who were engaged in intellectual

pursuits profited from studying the artists as they worked. Schools know nothing about this. The reason is that the educational process consists precisely in snuffing out the child's taste for the artist's methods, which seem disorderly on the surface, in order to teach him schedules and rules and good habits. But as one reaches man's estate, it is good to know that there are many ways of working other than those of the classroom and of childhood.

The painters, architects and other artists at the camp lived in very picturesque quarters; they had converted a laundry into a studio, and covered the walls with frescoes. As I remember, you saw Aphrodite rising from the waves, and there were other bravura flights of fancy. The washtub had been covered over and turned into a huge table for the architects. I used to stand by and admire their work; it teaches you so much about what will and intelligence, so closely joined in the artist, can create. It is quite impossible to produce an architectural work without envisaging an hypothesis that possesses not only noble and practical qualities but also irremediable deficiencies. The decision, therefore, to translate plan into fact represents in part a sacrifice. The architect cannot achieve everything; if he opts for façade, he will have to economize on the rear of the building, and be prepared to camouflage the more pedestrian details. The architect's freedom of choice lies in other areas entirely; in his as in all cases, to want one thing implies not to want something else—that is, to accept limitations, for without them action is impossible. The Cathedral of Notre Dame is the result of a decision made by a judicious will from among many equally possible solutions.

Another characteristic of artists is that generally they can only work in the fever of last-minute pressure; it is the pressure that forces them to finish a work. I suspect that if they didn't have to meet a deadline, they would dally indefinitely. For the architect there is that wonderful stint that comes at the last and which is entirely a matter of geometry; inspiration is suspended and the decision, which now has been taken, is developed and translated onto great sheets of paper in measurements exactly to scale, which will guide the contractor and the construction worker, and out of which will rise a three-dimensional creation capable of resisting the elements and the wear and tear of use, and which will be beautiful to look at in its every aspect. You should imitate these solid artists and never be satisfied with vague projects but force them through to precise and concrete solutions—the way military men must formulate battle orders. The student should hand in a clean, properly spelled and punctuated essay; the writer should *publish* —let himself be seen front, back, and profile, like an elegant woman whose dress and grooming are perfect to the last detail. The architect and the soldier are forced to this final perfecting of detail, of course, for otherwise the battle is lost or the house collapses.

This brings me to speak of actors, for the camp fostered many of them, too, quite as wonderfully good as they were unknown.

These were no drama-school graduates who did honor to our prison camp. But our actors had other qualities and advantages that professionals often lack: an inherited knowledge of the ways of the world; culture; uninterrupted time to themselves; a monastic life; suffering; the desire to help others rather than to make a name for themselves; total application to their role for months at a time. These things gave them the basis of dramatic art, which does not consist in recitation, but which is the faculty of achieving physical and emotional empathy

with this *other* man whom one is playing. It is known
that Molière and Shakespeare owed a part of their
genius to the fact that they lived in the company of
their actors, that they fathered their plays in the midst
of difficulties and under pressure, writing at white heat,
testing the words of their characters on a lower-class
public. I had to live in the close intimacy of a group,
in an almost monastic companionship, and in extreme
poverty, with no concern for success, in order to understand the kind of support, love, and art this manner of
life entails.

It was not a question for our actors of performing in
an existing theater, but of building a theater out of old
lumber, of constructing scenery and fashioning costumes
out of odds and ends, of rehearsing (on a near-starva-
tion diet), and of making intelligible to a very mixed
public not the facile stuff of a modern play but the
obscurities of a classical or symbolic play, like "Joan of
Arc" or "The Tidings Brought to Mary." Watching our
group of players, which included an architect, an artil-
leryman, a priest, and various others, I saw how the
primary art of comedy embraced many others, and that
there is no better exercise to perfect the memory—the
nerve of understanding—or to integrate mind and body,
or to arrive at the absolute in effort and achievement
than doing all this in a spirit of joy. I began to see why
the spirit in which those actors were working should be
transplanted, insofar as possible, into all activity. Work
is never better carried out than by a group, for then
each person escapes the anguish and pride of solitude,
and profits from the work of others.

But I also noticed that some of our actor troupes
were a group in appearance only—as happens often
with certain social groups—because the actors were
merely automatons in the hands of a director or walk-

ons clustered around a star. In those cases, everyone was submerged by the play and we did not even know the actors' names.

We should, I told myself, re-establish as widely as possible this pattern of teams working together. We have not been concerned enough with teaching children how to *work together* on a well-chosen focus of interest to all. When that is done, it is remarkable how the pride that human beings rightly take in work is based less on the individual task than on the common achievement, in which we take a healthy satisfaction entirely devoid of the sense of superiority that tends to isolate and depress us. And suddenly I remembered that once before, a long time ago, when I was teaching a group of illiterate enlisted men, I asked one of them to say in his own words what courage means. He got up and after a moment he said, "Courage, that's when somebody says . . . when somebody says to the rest, 'Listen, fellows, this is what we're going to do.' " In teamwork each person finds support in his neighbor, and, as in any co-operative effort, it is *A* who sees what has to be done and *B* who does it. To everyone his role.

## IV

People who work with their minds could learn a great deal from associating with military men.

I am not thinking of work methods, which in armies are always practical, efficient and concise, and which evidence a concern to pour all minds into a single mold so that any one can be quickly replaced. The rest of an army carries out what its commanding general, in whom genius is no drawback, has planned. This implies the subordination of every soldier to the whole, and

an impersonal method of discipline that raises the mediocre man above his usual level and obliterates individual
differences. An army is a school of collective, efficient
thought. And yet, paradoxical as it may seem, no profession is more favorable to thought than soldiering,
because it alternates the most intense action and absolute leisure, forces one to confront danger and the unforeseeable, as well as pure chance, and imposes on one
a wide range of tasks. It is a very free life where the
imagination, which discipline usually curbs at so many
points, may expand in a variety of dreams, in which
serious thoughts find nourishment in carefree ones; this
is the freedom enjoyed by the man who does not know
what tomorrow will bring but who has made up his
mind what the worst can be, and does not doubt that
it will come to pass. In this the military profession is a
mirror of the intellectual office: the secret, I think, is
to make yourself carry out very precise plans but at
the same time to leave yourself a wide margin of lib-
erty; to establish some very clear directions for your
activity but to allow for a measure of chance; not to
know exactly where you will arrive but to know nonetheless that you will get there.

For someone who works entirely with the mind it
would be a boon to have as a friend a man who is a
worker, or one who must on occasion risk his life. The
drawback in the intellectual professions is that the mistakes you make are not necessarily cause for dismay or
dishonor; on the contrary, as Descartes pointed out,
often it is your mistakes that bring you fame and credit.
The shoemaker who turns a bad heel has the advantage
of being punished forthwith: his customer doesn't come
back. But people who engage in pure intellectual pursuits generally do so without risk to themselves. I have
often thought that what some people relish in freedom

of opinion is their certainty that they need not answer for their ideas with their own skins. True, this is not always so, in which case intellectual labor will remind you that there is a resemblance between the pen and the sword. Renan had this in mind when, as an old man, he said he wished that great dreamers would have to work as navy torpedoists; it would give them, he said, "the means of dreaming serenely on in this world except that now and then, for a few heroic moments, they would face up to the chances of not coming out of the thing alive." In such an outlook we rediscover the principle on which noble rank once rested: men who had the advantage of being dukes of the realm held that advantage because their life blood was always at the disposition of their king.

I will venture a few more details about what I learned from associating with military men.

When you are in the company of monks or priests or army men, you are always surprised at how extremely free their ideas are—I mean their ideas about the very things they profess to revere. André Maurois has given some fine examples of this in "Silences" and in "Marshal Lyautey." A pure intellectual, on the other hand, is scarcely able to criticize without lapsing into a scornful tone. The *dedicated* man has greater ease in perceiving calmly and clearly what his cause may lack.

More than any other mental effort, military life renews and by extension rejuvenates the mind. Usually, in the liberal professions, we are always doing the same thing. Herein lies the risk of our too soon wearing out and losing the ability to widen our experience. Because our modern armies are being constantly made over, the professional military man, even a general, must sit down at a desk now and then to study and learn a new trade. Americans are right in thinking that we can change our way of living more than once—be born again at forty, or at sixty go back and finish school.

I also observed, in that enforced prison solitude, future statesmen and diplomats who, heeding the advice

"To find out what you cannot do
And then to go and do it,"

used to get together to study as a group under the leadership of some comrade who was already launched in a public service career.

Their "school" was fashioned from a room similar to the one used by the artists and the sink also had been turned into a big table. It made me think that the first work tool, whether for architect, strategist or diplomat, is a table on which he can spread things out. The competitive examinations certifying a man for government service will always have one thing in common: they test the applicant not so much on his formal knowledge as on his skill in setting forth a subject, in not letting himself be trapped in debate, and in convincing his opponent or listener.

For people in government service, intellectual work difficulties derive from the existence of the Written Law. Between their intelligences and the problem at hand is interposed such a screen of precedents and statutes that what they need even more than knowledge is ingenuity. They must evaluate a situation not by seeing it as it is but by applying to it some earlier regulation that had never been devised to fit the present instance. This is a habit one does not acquire in youth, yet it could be a subject for study even at an early age. We have a notion that the humanities and the sciences are the only disciplines that can form a young mind, and that the study of law—although at the outset this is analogous to material studied in the secondary schools—should be postponed until after the bachelor's degree. Knowledge of law, however, is a source of experience that can develop your judgment and familiarize you with what justice is. If a people (as, for example, the French) lack a civic sense, that is perhaps due to the fact that nobody ever told them early in life just what the Law is.

## V

In the course of postwar vicissitudes, I went back to work at the high-school level and I would like to say what I learned from that. This return to teaching less advanced classes was for me a happy experience. I do wish the same could happen to more people, that the colonel become a sergeant again, or the engineer a foreman—on one condition, that is: that the step downward be taken without bitterness, since resentment would prevent the man's benefiting from it.

The ideal, if you are to re-form yourself, would be, somewhere in middle age, to have to teach a bright young boy or girl. Without having to be otherwise responsible for him, that is. In this way, you would teach everything and would be able to watch your student actually perceiving all the interconnections. Bossuet was forty-three years old when he became tutor to the Dauphin who was to become Louis XIV. For the sake of the child-king, this churchman, uninstructed in mundane things, had to learn law, physics, and physiology. He rekindled long-quenched areas in his own recollections of history, and did this at an age when one finally knows what history is about.

Sometimes I go as an observer when one of the less rigorous formal examinations is being given, such as

those for the bachelor's degree or the teaching certifi-
cate, just in order to sound out the depths of what
I myself do not know. Who among us professors would
emerge from such examinations with honor? When I
question students in class, I often ask myself privately,
"Would I always be able to answer the questions I put
to them?" The difference between the man and the
boy is that the latter is not authorized to ask questions,
only the young Jesus having taken this right upon Himself before the learned scribes.

A classroom is a good source of discipline, for its
pre-established schedule is as precise as the sun's. There
is a quieting effect in the regular pattern of movements,
the almost liturgical monotony, and the long, attentive
silences. It is amusing at the same time, because you
always find fluctuations: the stars of the class; the indescribable dunces who are so funny to watch; and
that solid core of middle-of-the-roader's, docile sheep
dominated by some ram. The classroom connects you
with the larger order of society, too, through the unexpected visits of a principal, come to make some special
announcement, or an inspector, who brings a breath
from the outer world into that agreeable and even
sleepy atmosphere.

When I came back to the high-school world, I found
it exactly as it had been on my leaving it as a student,
fifteen years before. The same people playing the same
parts, even to the boy who read the roll and the "stove
boy," who, in winter, stuffed coal into the same old
stove. You would have said that no progress—no re-
gression, either—had been able to alter the venerable
structure of the French classroom in which the tradi-
tion of the Jesuits, the mentality of emperors, and all
our lay habits have been reconciled.

The room I taught in was one of the poorest ever.

Windowpanes that had been broken during bombard-
ments of the city had been replaced by cardboard, so
that the room was dark indeed. The principal explained
to me that this closing-off of the view was an excellent
thing; it prevented the town women from looking down
into the room as they swept their balconies and, even
better, it put an end to the students' ogling back. It
was a room in authentic Napoleonic style, situated in a
former monastery, and furnished chiefly with a few
indolent students whom I found prepared for that
perpetual semi-snooze that is not, after all, so awfully
disagreeable.

I tried to revamp my methods of teaching: What, I
asked myself, could I do for them and for me, given
my surplus of knowledge, their basic ignorance, their
entirely reasonable concern to pass their final examination, and the need for a genuine culture, which they
also felt. At every turn I met the same problem of routine. Too heavy programs, on one hand, and sullen-
ness on the students' part, as a result. There were summer afternoons when I was caught by surprise to hear
my own voice droning on about philosophy—which was
not preventing me from thinking of something quite
different. The dutiful fountain pens were sawing away
like so many crickets, and the minds of the boys were
wandering among dreams far more colorful than mine.
To wake us all up, I used to prefer to entertain them
or talk with them, or even tell them about some inci-
dent in my own life. When it was a question of work,
I wanted it to be work at peak performance. But I
took care to call a halt at the least sign of fatigue. The
troupe had to be on its toes or else really relaxed. I well
realize that this is tantamount to condemning many current teaching methods. But how painful it is to drop
in on a so-called study hall. Fine in principle, but who-

ever sits down beside the students to teach them how
to make real use of a dictionary, or how to organize a
paper? No one, and so they work away unremittingly
on mathematics, copying the answers to problems from
the better students.

I know very well that a radical change in the world
of the well-deserving professors and the assistants who
supervise the study hall in our boarding schools would
imply a sweeping reorganization of the entire system.
We have set up our classes admirably: we offer ten-
year-old students a roster of full professors who, in other
countries, would be teaching in the universities. The
competitive examinations that certify us to teach in
lyceums and universities—and that permit us to earn
a modest living—are among the most difficult in the
world. The students cannot complain: in this sense,
they have been so well provided for that it never occurs to them—nor do their parents suspect—that the
professors are indifferent to their pupils' studies. The
professor is at the *lycée* only for the hours of his classes.
The rest of the time the student is on his own, yet here
is precisely where he needs help.

I tried also in my own teaching to abolish the aristo-
cratic rule that dictates the approach of most young
professors, that is, to teach the class for the benefit of
the best students in it. I have always tried to open the
closed mind and the slow mind, in the belief that if
we teachers can get results with middling students, the
élite would be given unto us as well. Socrates used to
talk to the common people of Athens, and Plato was
given to him.

My idea was to teach by the simplest methods possible and to get positive results sooner rather than later.
I used to make rather few corrections on student papers,
for I myself had grown tired of all those little red marks

in the margin that nobody ever reread. But I did search through the paper for some significant error; then I would take the student aside and teach him the rule he had broken, and that particular mistake I did not allow him to repeat. Or, on the other hand, I would single out the good or promising passage in a paper (you almost always find one) so that the student became aware of his ability and learned to imitate himself at his best. Generally, we proceed on the basis of what is wrong, we point out the error, as if every exercise had a right or wrong, like arithmetic and spelling. But we could just as well do the reverse and encourage the good to conquer the bad. What a pleasure it is, in a school, to see a vacant, morose, and rather sullen face suddenly light up at such recognition—without, however, the student's giving up one iota of the insolence that is considered indispensable in our free world of today.

## VI

In all its aspects, intellectual work is related to our inner life. Intellectuality—I mean mental power—should not be separated from spiritual strength. We have lost any sense of the relationship between the intelligence and the soul, and suffer today from the separation that we have allowed to develop between technique and spirit. What we have preserved is the mentality of the slave. We make a sharp distinction between our professional duties, which for most of us are the means of guaranteeing our subsistence, and the pleasures of leisure in which we enjoy total freedom. And it must be admitted that it is virtually impossible to find a niche for the mind in the inhuman jobs available in our industrial and administrative enterprises—that is, in the mechanical, monotonous motions that such jobs involve. People are obliged to hand themselves over body and soul to the machine or to the public, eight hours a day, as if they were living an automated dream. We lend ourselves to such work without putting any part of ourselves into it, unless it be a measure of boredom or irritation. Some types of work, thank God, still preserve areas of freedom. And there are still some fine occupations that are work in the sense of the word's earliest meaning—the performing of a service or a moral duty.

The trade of the intellectual—especially for you who are at the searching stage—is one of the most free and beautiful that can be offered to you in the first splendid flowering of your youth. In certain quite profound ways, it is remarkably analogous to the work of the farmer, and Vergil, I think, in the Georgics, sensed this connection. It escaped the editors of the New Testament, who were not writers for all that they gave a fine example of how to say much in few words. But how these mysterious parables could be transposed into guides for the mind's work, for style and inspiration! For example, the mustard seed, smallest of all seeds, that once planted grows silently until it becomes a perch for the birds of heaven; or the sower who gives most of his grain for the one kernel that germinates and yields a hundredfold; or the field in which weed and crop are so intermingled that one must wait for the harvest to sort them out; or the advice to let the earth lie fallow so that it may restore itself.

In a way, the observations and reflections that follow are merely comments on these first principles. The job of tilling the soil, like the job of the soldier or sailor, offers food for the spirit; the only question is to extract it. The same is true for voluntary study:

*Ingressum instruas*
*Progressum custodias*
*Egressum impleas.*

You might translate this prayer of St. Thomas thus: "Look after the preparations/Survey the progress/Harvest the fruits." The prayer suggests the rhythm of this little book, in which you try to let yourself be borne on by the rhythm of the human mind engaged in an intellectual effort. You may think of it as the movement of a wave that gathers itself together, rises, swells, and breaks, leaving its mark upon the sand.

# 2

# Preparation

# of Work

It seems that the first bit of advice that should be given the person who works is: try to know yourself. This is not to say that you should clasp your head between your hands and plunge into the inner depths of your being, where you see nothing. It means you should review in your mind what you have done during the past week, counting up the hours in which you worked well, seeing where you failed and where you succeeded. It is very necessary to recognize your own strong points, because—the most foolish ideas being those in widest circulation—curricula and study plans abound that would make you believe you can all acquire positively encyclopedic knowledge.

School teaches us to talk in terms of allusions to something we know nothing about. (This is the supreme art of the orator, guaranteeing him considerable success.) You will go on doing this in later life, for, after all, it is not distasteful. The day you are sure you can no longer be examined on what you do not know, you feel very much relaxed; if you are able to talk about a given subject, that will be quite enough. Read a few books, know when to maintain an astute silence, be able to launch a few brisk sallies against points you've brushed up on in advance, and you can hold your own in this world. If it were necessary to know everything, you would invite disgrace by not knowing. But just cast up the working hours left in a man's life after deducting time for sleep, essential physical care, traveling back and forth, routine chores, and so forth, and you will see how very little time remains for the mind's work, even if you devote yourself to that primarily— and here I am speaking of basic work that mobilizes your deepest resources. You have only to live side by side with an intellectual in prison to notice that, after all, he possesses rather little knowledge at his immediate disposition and must have recourse to books or to a long preliminary preparation. The intelligence of such a man differs from average minds in that what it knows it utilizes with elegance. It manipulates its capital marvelously well. M. Benrubi published a book on his conversations with Henri Bergson over a period of thirty years. What struck me in this book was seeing how a great mind was able to adapt one answer to fit widely varying questions. Goethe did the same with Eckermann. And who would dream of criticizing this? The merit of the mind does not reside so much in its being learned (the reference books are always at hand) as in its being lively—vital enough to adapt its knowledge and principles to whatever is new or unique, and, inversely, quick to sense how it can derive nourishment from each and every thing chance brings its way. Observing the work of an artist is one of the best ways to detect this mixture of poverty and wealth, which is the lot of the whole human race. It is striking that the portraits an artist has painted of very different subjects strangely resemble each other. This is because art precedes any meeting between the artist's spirit and a specific external reality. The painter is not formed by studying innumerable objects but by choosing and considering those he has felt in harmony with in advance. He reworks these subjects according to his own lights. For this reason, it matters relatively little to true artists that their subject matter be extraordinary or noble; they are better pleased with a subject that appears insignificant. You can observe the same trait in saints.

One exceptional thing about Marcel Proust's work is the fact that the material he transfigured was intrinsically so devoid of interest—memories such as any sensitive child preserves, the chatter of idle, worldly people. His ingenuity lay in understanding that the more banal the material, the more evident the talent, and that so noticeable a contrast would make the reader sense the very functioning of art, which it is so agreeable to detect throbbing under the surface of a masterpiece, like its own breathing.

Great men are made of no different stuff than you people are. All of you have to carry out tasks, some of which are easy and some difficult, and all must remain alert while performing routine jobs. And to watch people endowed with genius at work throws light on your own small chores.

Say that the problem is to prepare for a final examination, or to work on a composition, or to write some poems that will never be shown to a soul. What urges the young student on is—in kind—the same thing a great author relies on. I would even go so far as to say that you as a young person enjoy certain advantages over the mature person—leisure, a basic confidence in yourself, and freedom from those moments of doubt that darken the spirit.

The first thing to remember is the great law of the

will that counsels you to choose and then to persist.

In his "Rules," Descartes said that the whole of method consists "in the order and disposition of that toward which the attention must be directed in order to perceive some truth therein." The human mind is powerful but often perplexed; when finally it knows what it should be concerned with and toward what goal it should be aiming, it is greatly reassured. The heaviest burden for the spirit is not to know what should be done. Once you have made a choice, you can endure losing everything you possess or stand up to any hostility or opposition. You are no longer suffering from uncertainty. This faculty of attention is what you mean, really, when you say "mind." And it is quite appropriate for you to compare attention to a point—*acies mentis,* or "aim of the mind," Descartes called it—or to represent it by an inverted cone. As attention is mobilized and fixes on a given thing, it becomes stronger. This is a simple but harsh truth that your way of life, education, and native indolence make you overlook.

Intellectual work that you are allowed to perform mechanically resembles what in old-fashioned military strategy was called "the parallel battle." This means that you do not choose a site and concentrate your efforts there but allow your troops to be engaged everywhere. In terms of our discussion, this is equivalent to wanting to know everything. The battle tactic that is conceived as the total application of your forces against certain pre-established points is suggestively similar to the concentration of attention on the knotty core of a problem.

"There are a lot of good generals in Europe," Napoleon was fond of saying, "but they see too many things. I see masses, and that is what I attack, for I am sure that secondary elements will fall of themselves." Elsewhere he said, "Everything becomes simple, easy,

defined, nothing is vague, when the central point of a
country has been long established on the basis of a
superior authority. One realizes how the existence of
such a central point makes for order and security." And
again: "It is not with large numbers of troops but with
well-organized and well-disciplined troops that one wins
a war." In the realm of intellectual work these principles
would imply maxims such as: Know which things to
neglect; do not try to comprehend everything; attach
yourself to one maypole and dance around it.


## II


The same line of reasoning implies that you must
make a sharp distinction between the phases of preparation, execution, and rest. You must never allow these
phases to become jumbled together, never be content
with the kind of aimless activity that is neither relaxation nor application—the kind many students and bu-
reaucrats are satisfied to settle for. In army life, long
periods of sluggishness suddenly give way to a fever of
brief, intense action that in turn lapses back into relaxation. Manuals of physical education, a form of discipline in which one is required to perform sensibly, say
that the athletic director must demand a sustained effort from his group or else call for time out: "There is
no in-between situation."

The golden rule of intellectual work can be put thus:
tolerate neither half-work nor half-rest. Give yourself
totally *or* withhold yourself absolutely. Never allow the
two to overlap.

This is an implicit criticism of several school pro-
cedures. Go into a high school or college, visit a student's
room or an administrator's office, and you will often
find this rule being broken. The drowsy classes, the

dismal dormitory-barracks, the enforced attendance—
all these contribute to learning how to half-work, which
is a total of waste time and destroys any pleasure in
either effort or relaxation. Poor thinking mankind! I
asked a teacher once, "Why do you keep them in study
hall so long?" And he, honest man, answered, "A study
hall is easier to supervise than a recreation period."

A well-known philosopher, Simone Weil (1909-1943),
speaking of attention, said once that it "is an effort,
perhaps the greatest of all efforts, but yet a negative
one. In itself it does not induce fatigue. When fatigue
sets in, it becomes almost impossible to focus the attention unless one has been well trained. So, at that point
it is better to give up, find some form of relaxation
and recoup one's energies, and after a while, begin
afresh. In other words, one should disengage oneself,
then presently pick up and go on. It's rather like breathing in and breathing out." The attention she is talking
about presupposes a most perfect and bland state that,
interestingly enough, the mind resists even more violently
than the body revolts against fatigue. It is a state of
pure waiting, in which the mind refrains from hurling
itself upon a sham truth but is willing to wait to receive
a genuine truth. Simone Weil says that misinterpreta-
tions in translation or absurd solutions to mathematical
problems are causd by this greediness of the attention,
which is unable to relax and wait.

Some people let themselves slip into actual illness
to avoid having to act with true courage and patience.
Others hide behind a screen of overwork to evade the
concentration they detest or the relaxation which would
bring them face to face with themselves. How often
have you heard: "I don't know which way to turn
next. . . . I sleep six hours at the very most." How
good it would be to hear instead: "I enjoy my work.
. . . I've got free time—time for myself."

So you must discriminate between the chore—that is, an activity in which the mind need not involve itself fully—and work, to which you give yourself as completely as you can. The latter brings with it both joy and pain, as does everything to which you give yourselves totally, and it alone deserves to be called by the hard name of work. Jules Payot, a great educator, was right to say that "the time span of true work is short." He challenged examples, often cited, of great workers in the field of literature; he showed that what they termed "work" often consisted in a brewing, a stirring, a kind of erudite torpor—in other words, in what makes the web of all housekeeping-like activity, which can be summed up in that fine word "chore."

Payot talks about Zola and Flaubert; he shows you those giants working ten hours at a clip. Not that they were then making a sustained creative effort; rather, they had learned how to mechanize a particular phase of work, or they were pondering the choice of the best word. Choosing involves the exercise of taste, which in turn requires a great deal of indolence and of time wisely lost. Intensity would spoil everything. Do not become confused. Neither the chore nor the act of discernment is work in the pure sense in which I use the word; by work I mean total mobilization of your being. It is important, at least for you beginners, never to mislead yourselves into calling effort that which is only a caricature of effort, or preparation for it, or the trail toward it. Preparing the stage for a drama is not the same as acting in that drama.

You should strive, then, to discover what are your royal hours, the hours when attention is lucid, penetrating, and in most lively harmony with the self. You should chart these hours of active peace, determine how many there are, how long they last, what their rhythm is, in what pattern they come and go, and then make your work revolve around them. During those hours you should never let yourselves be caught up by the trivialities of the outside world. You should revolutionize your schedule (getting up at five or going to bed at ten, say) in order to make your work revolve around the axis of these sacred hours, and not treat time on a catch-as-catch-can basis. Unfortunately, it becomes less and and less possible for you to be masters of your own time. The spirit if not the letter of this program can be lived up to, however. To avoid overwork, you must determine which are the hours when you are fresh; use them for what is most urgent or most demanding or most divinely agreeable; give to them that human manna known as your "best," and leave the rest to God to make up for any deficiencies.

People differ on this point. Some work better in the morning; they get up with the sun, or before. The moral philosophers of classical times countenanced no exception to the rule that man—all men—works with a will in the early morning hours. The religious orders have preserved this dictum. But in modern life everything starts so late that it is very hard to go to bed at sundown with the monks; evenings offer the greatest privacy, ease, and mystery, all of which suggests going to bed later, and getting up later. Furthermore, the nervous temperaments which abound more and more in today's world often cannot really go to sleep until the small hours and their mornings drag because, with them, mind and body reaccustom themselves to each other very slowly.

You must also learn that the potential of your attention varies. It can rarely be both total and focused and sustain itself in this state for two consecutive hours. The Apocalypse speaks of a period of silence in heaven which Bossuet said lasted half an hour; here on earth it would be much shorter! Often everything blurs after twenty minutes, and then the tired mind works against itself. But even a man who cannot concentrate for more than ten minutes at a time—like Montaigne, who by nature was quick-witted ("What I don't see on the first charge," he said, "I see even less well by persisting")— even such a man could accomplish a great deal if he would pause and then apply himself afresh, like rowers who rest for a fraction of a second after each stroke. The important thing is to know and to accept yourself; to have taken a sounding of your own strength, as if you were testing a piece of machinery; to know the degree of attention you are capable of; to know at what times of day it is at its peak, when it falls off, and when it should be recharged by rest or a change of work or by play. This curve of your personal endurance span should be as present to you as atmospheric readings are to the transoceanic pilot.

## III

The arrangements you make for a place in which to work and for some kind of companionship are as important as your management of time.

You need only look about you to see how habits differ here. Some need an atmosphere surpeopled with books, papers, and a disorder in the midst of which, as Victor Hugo put it, their inspiration "squats." Others have an equal need of order composed of elimination and emptiness; these people keep only essentials around them. Some—the German lyric poet Rilke was one— must have a very small room, like a monk's cell, and a nondescript view that turns them back upon themselves, while, on the other hand, there are people—like the philosopher Sertillanges—who need an expanse of mountain or sea.

Preparation for work includes making a nest—or better, creating the right atmosphere.

Your first care, I believe, should be to find a refuge, a corner, some little place to yourself—and that is to be found even in prison. Fix up this little cave; that is, make it the kind of place in which everything is at once calm and stimulating. If a room is luxuriously furnished, let it be at least a sober luxury. If your circumstances are instead straitened, let your poverty be full of symbols. Tolerate nothing near you, Ruskin said, that you do not find either useful or beautiful. Applied to a work area, this rule involves several do's and don't's.

It is good to know where the light comes from. The slanting rays of the late afternoon sun may be helpful, or morning light, or summer light filtering through the blinds. The same holds for a lamp, and particularly for the lamp shade, which creates a cone of light, the style of which can also be chosen to your own taste. When possible, there should be a second being or creature acting both as resister and reflector, for this helps you control your burgeoning ideas, rather in the manner of the confidant in classical tragedy.

It is undeniably hard to find a collaborator of this sort, docile enough yet also sufficiently mirror-like to be your projected better self. The admiration that someone feels for you helps clear away many stumbling blocks. A secretary or a nontalkative disciple, or a wife who knows when to be quiet, can render this greatly needed service. You find the aides you deserve. Is there anyone who does not have some helpful companion within hailing distance—a cat who wakes to stretch and stare at you with its inhuman eyes; or a sleeping child; or a student who asks you to please unravel for him some enormous knots that for you do not exist?

## IV

When you read the lives of various great men—of all great men, perhaps, if the account is truthful—you will notice that the conditions of their childhood, their education, or their profession did not predispose them to what they ultimately accomplished. It is not *because* of their education, it is often *in spite* of it that they were able to develop. This man grew up without books, that man had to study secretly. It makes you wonder what the word "advantages" really means, what parents mean when they say they want their children to have all the advantages they themselves did not have. Do you ever know what is for you an advantage? Is not the lack of something often most helpful? For the lack of an external thing arouses an inner impulse that replaces it; the "I," the individual's native gift, is substituted. Every time an outer support is replaced by an impulse that comes from within you are on the road to a renewal of self and of the world. So you need never pity people who complain that they lack this or that, *provided* they have pledged themselves to reach their goal.

You do have to set out before everything is ready, otherwise you would never get up the steam to move. I was once told that the philosopher Renouvier suffered from a peculiar type of deafness that is lessened in the midst of noise. To make people suffering from this kind of impaired hearing catch what you say, you have to speak to the rattle of drums. The best thing to do with Renouvier, it appears, was to go with him to watch the train roar in and out of the station in the little town of Prades; during those fifteen noisy minutes, communication was possible.

Certain types of intelligence suffer from an analogous paradox. For their heads to function, they need a contrary occupation. When André Vincentaire, the hero of "Patrice de la Tour du Pin," is rehearsing "La contemplation errante," he works even in cafés, for, he says, "If I am not brave there, when will I ever be?"

It is good to be alone while you work, far removed from noise. Yet I know people who need a rhythm, sometimes an indistinct noise. A crowd helps them; passing figures, or the sound of children at play or of dishwashing, have become so useful to them that if they were deprived of this accompaniment they could not work. Maybe that was Descartes' idea in fleeing from the country where one cannot escape from inconvenient neighbors and preferring to live in the great Dutch city of Amsterdam with its spectacle of human labor and diversely regulated activity. Anatole France said, "Tumult is necessary to me. When I am alone, I read. When I am disturbed, I cannot read and so I write." Paul Valéry extolled the help that is to be found in the bustle of a busy port.

The most favorable conditions are not always the best, so likely are you to spoil what you have in superabundance. How do you explain the fact that university people, whose job it is to think and to write, produce less lasting work than amateurs who write on the side as a kind of pastime? The novelist André Maurois is a businessman; A. J. Cronin, a doctor; Bruce Marshall, at one time, an accountant; Claudel was a diplomat who might have said, together with Lamartine, that poetry took up no more of his time than praying or breathing; Graham Greene was once a journalist; the late John F. Kennedy was a politician who found time to write a prize-winning historical study; Guillaumin, a laboring, harvesting peasant. Descartes claimed to have made his major discoveries amid the bustle of military camps; Spencer was an engineer; Winston Churchill, as we know, spent a lifetime in his government service; Thomas Merton is a Trappist monk. Even the spectacle of stupidity, as mindless and inexhaustible as wind or sea, should be able to help you.

A regular occupation that does not demand too much tension but that requires you to perform certain duties without being deeply involved in them—for example, a subaltern officer or secondary schoolteacher—can often provide restful support for your own intellectual work. The essential thing is not to be too absorbed, which, sad to say, becomes more and more difficult. Novalis said, "The more eager the mind is to be tranquil and active, the better it is for a man to try to engage his body in unimportant activities. It is like grounding a negative wire in order to be more positively active and productive."

# 3

# The Profound

# Effort

Delacroix once remarked to Baudelaire, "Art is so visionary and fugitive a thing that one's tools are never clean enough or one's methods quick enough." Suppose that, insofar as possible, you have completed your preparations and are face to face with the task that has been put to you—reading, editing an article, writing a long novel, carrying out some art project, it doesn't matter which; all mental labor is much alike. At this point, temptations raise their heads and even seem to cue each other: you look about for a pen; read the newspaper; listen to street noises; check on a few references; reminisce about the last war; make a telephone call; recall something you said or some professor said; dream about vacation; consider parceling out the work to subordinates; smoke; doublecheck a bill; lapse into clichés; lose your temper; decide to wait for a moment of inspiration; delay; postpone; give up. It is useful to itemize all these ambiguous devils; you cannot banish them all—and some are actually a proper part of your work—but you must know their faces so that you are not tricked by any of their disguises.

Here, as always happens when it is a question of effort, the powers, good, bad and indifferent, league together against you. What gives temptation its strength is not its grimacing evil but the smiling goodness that is fused with it. That is why you must hurry along, must eliminate as much as possible having to get down to business. There is no such thing as preliminaries in work or in love.

## II

But what does intellectual effort consist of?

I think that it is a question of moving from one plane to another. Your intelligence tends to confine itself to the plane of ideas alone or of facts alone. Actually, the thing that should arrest your attention is a fact illuminated by an idea or an idea incarnated in a fact. This is the vital principle of science. The pure fact does not exist; the proper object of your search is not pure fact but the fact insofar as it refers you to a general law. In the same way, a pure, abstract law is not conceivable; the law must synthesize a multitude of facts. In a drawing there is no generalized line; it is the curve of that nose, the modulation of those lips, the roll of those hills on the horizon that you try to capture. If drawing were only a matter of recopying such and such kind of learned line, it would require no effort of you except to get started. But what the artist does is something quite different from remembering. He seeks to create a particular line, which he senses will not exist twice.

Once upon a time, a professor of rhetoric reduced all past and all possible future dissertations to five major types. He taught his students these five great categories. The day they took their final examination, they had only to decide, after a moment's reflection, whether

Class A or Class C was called for, and fire away from the appropriate battery.

I know of mathematics professors who proceed in the same way, and there would be no reason to criticize the method provided their students try to adapt the general type to the particular; that is, adapt it to the new circumstances that are proposed to them. Such adaptation is the end of art and the mark of intelligence. In military science you can see a lazy tendency to try to make a concrete problem fit some old strategic plan learned in school. Truth and validity are not to be found by this tactic, which is the very opposite of method. "Let us dispense with all automatic solutions," Foch used to tell his classes at the War College. "Let us first have general principles, then let us apply these principles to the case at hand, which is always new and fresh, and let us keep asking ourselves the question that the mind tends to neglect: What is the objective?" These maxims from the art war apply also to the art of living. Examinations, which are, figuratively, battles, are also won and lost by such expedients; how many corpses litter the field of battle because students do not understand the question they are asked to discuss or because, having once understood it, they fail to adapt their knowledge to it, or because they rattle off some old formula or idea without relating it to the topic at issue—in other words, because they avoid making an effort. Failures that are explained away as being due to chance are, most of the time, failures due to nerves or to giving up without having tried.

When I express a thought in speech or writing, what is the nature of that effort? It is clear that first I have a broad, dim notion of what I am going to say; otherwise, I should never be able to begin. But this broad idea is not a detailed plan; it is not an outline I have prepared into which I can slot words one by one until it is fleshed out. My broad idea acts like a current of air that catches up particles of dust, the way a magnet attracts iron filings, the way an arm is extended to point out a direction. And as within yourself you soundlessly utter this wordless thought, the spoken words begin to fall from your lips. To be accurate, the process is more complex than this; for the spoken word, through consonance and through the association of ideas and images that it carries with it, suggests how you should change or correct or amplify, so that while you do not suppress the interior model, you do modify it in numerous ways and make it more precise and rich. And so it is that as you speak on, you know better and better what it was you did want to say—and no doubt that is quite different from what you first planned to say. Think for a moment of great public speakers, men like the aforementioned Winston Churchill and even the demoniac Adolf Hitler, who rushed headlong into the adventure of speech, and who began to talk (as in ordinary life all of you do) without knowing how the flood would unroll or on what shore it might touch. Most professionals know that the first words of a sentence build a flexible scaffolding and that if they are to avoid a pause or break, they must let themselves be borne easily along by the rhythm of the phrase, their attention fixed partly on their idea, partly on the sounded words and their assonances, in a kind of waking dream that the merest nothing could interrupt. For if they think too hard about their idea, their words falter, their speech loses its wings, and the orator shrinks into the professor. If they let themselves be carried away by associations, they risk losing their train of thought.

The same holds true for the writer; what he writes is the more precious for not being formulated in advance and for making full use of the accidents of language. In poetry rhyme can be a means of invention, and it is the word itself that sumons another word to respond to it, as one color calls to another on the palette—not because the second color is found in the landscape but because it is wedded to the first by affinity or by contrast. In this respect poetry does not differ from written or spoken prose. All of which reminds you that in intellectual effort the art of discovery lies in this back-and-forth that leads you from the level of sound to the level of meaning and intention via a process of constant adjustment. I once heard a teacher give some good advice to a student who was asking him how to write his dissertation in seven hours: "Spend the first hour," the older man said, "studying the boundaries of your subject —weigh them, heft them, test them against each other. In other words, define them. It almost always happens that the question that has been put to you will emerge clear and distinct from this kind of exercise. Then make sure of your general direction. Have a plan rather than an outline. Then throw yourself headlong into writing; you will see that by themselves ideas will come to you at the right moment. And if someone says to you later that the organization of your paper is not perfect, say to yourself that no other organization would be perfect, either."

Here, it seems to me, is the way to solve the old familiar problem of writing a first draft and then revising and recopying. I've never thought it sound to spend time on a rough draft in a limited examination period. Much better first to reflect and then to launch at once into the adventure of writing. In the works of nature, form and substance issue from the same action. The work of a lifetime obeys this same rhythm. Plans are necessary, and success goes to those who take the long view. But the plan must remain supple and vacant, ready to bend, shrink, or expand in response to opportunities, obstacles, and your own meanderings. People of action observe their lives as well as manage them.

These examples, and you find them all around, suggest that effort resides in a median zone, to which the idea descends from its abode to become incarnate in a detail, in a specific instance, in a concrete thing; it is also and inversely the zone to which fact summons an idea in which it apprehends a meaning. These two motions, ascent and descent, are the breathing of the intelligence.

You have not gone far, it is true, if you stop with only these great principles. What is difficult in art is execution. It is impossible to teach people to be intelligent, but you can suggest in what direction they should look for intelligence to come to them.

### III

Where do you find the point of application?

"Give me a lever," Archimedes said.

Especially give him the crack into which he can insert his lever, and he will indeed be able to "move the earth."

In everything you must look for the fissure, the preformed groove in which you have only to adjust the lever, like wood-splitters who, once they have driven their wedge between the fibers of an oak, have almost solved their problem; the rest is a matter of their ax, strength, and chopping.

You are on the threshold of the mystery of the mind. How are you to account for the flair that *A* possesses and that *B* lacks? Why does one person see the crack straight off, while the other looks around for it desperately? How explain why one man promptly chooses a wrong spot and strikes against, rather than with the grain of the wood, whereas his companion unerringly follows the grain? Why do you see around you lives wasted on senseless activities and side by side with them those silent existences that seem to emanate the even more silent power that renews all things?

I knew a child once who was the despair of his parents because he could not understand arithmetic. The boy's father, graduate of the great Polytechnique, saw his escutcheon stained forever. But I knew that he could not teach his son. To the father it seemed that mistakes in arithmetic were the result of stupidity; they were a family disgrace. I was consulted. I am not familiar with the mysteries of mathematics, but I have the advantage of knowing why I am weak in this subject. My first teachers never explained to me what arithmetic was about, or where you had to tackle the problems; much less did they make it clear that the mystery is a matter of appearances only. One secret of mastering mathematics, at least in its early phases, is, I think, never to want to get to the bottom of the thing but to accept everything with surprise. The mistake is to look too hard; try to eliminate, simplify, replace unknown quantities with symbols; act as if the problem were already solved. Try each day's problem as it comes. Go at it from another angle. Sleep on it and try again in the morning, fresh. This is the geometrician's moral system. But you don't know this when you're in school.

You can also profit from the experience of others. You are not exploring virgin territory; men have gone before you and laid out the trails and marked the water holes. Probably they have also marked "the points of application" on the map. I remember how horrified I was when I heard that I would have to study the whole of Plato for my Master's degree. My professors read off the list of the editions of Plato that had appeared within the last twenty years; several were in foreign languages. Then they warned against summaries, abridged editions, and "ponies." Here they were quite right. But my problem was having to study Plato over a period of only a few months—months made up of twenty-four-hour-long days, in which sleep, eating, other reading, other study, and leisure, too, all had their rights. Inspiration led me to a teacher who detested anything conventional, and I went to see him one evening. He received me in his study, lined with books among which I recognized, in rank upon serried rank, the works of Plato. I told him what brought me: "Has one to read everything?" "Oh, my dear fellow!" he said. "Mind that you don't!" "Well, then," I asked, "should one read nothing?" "Take even more care not to do that," and he pointed out then that Plato had been read and reread by writers whom I was reading at the time; he said I should make a list of the passages in Plato that these authors mentioned, and then notice which were the most frequently quoted. He said these would be promontories—or lookouts, rather—from which my eye could range over different domains. Once these vantage points were marked off, he advised, I should stick with them; in other words, I should go back again and again to those particular passages in Plato and make them my "bible." Finally, he said, I would discover that their light would illuminate the context in which they were set, and the broader areas of the Dialogue as a whole, with all the neighboring and analogous passages, the flat spaces and the depressions, even the more obscure, almost impenetrable passages. The long sojourn upon the more accessible heights would throw some light even on these, he said. I found the lack of hypocrisy in his advice very much to my taste.

One cannot possibly repeat that beautiful natural law too often: in all things, proceed from the known to the unknown.

## IV

I have noticed, too, that geologists are often worth imitating, as, for example, when they are carefully observing areas where two distinct strata are found side by side. The transitions, the joints, the passage beds—in other words, the places where this stops being this and becomes that; the time of origin and the periods of change; all these have meaning. The composer realizes very keenly that the hardest part about composing is not so much thinking up ideas or themes as linking two themes or ideas by a passage that is not contrived. The artist's power shows itself in his capacity for making these transitions. In this respect, nature is a prodigious artist, hiding her mediations and passages from us under a seeming continuity. Anyone who settles down in a seam or joint may be lucky enough to penetrate some secret of creation.

In history, the periods that fascinate you are periods of transition and revolution. Military strategy directs you to attack the allied armies of the enemy at the point where their forces join. The same holds true for the battle in which the objective is self-truth. It is via connections and junctions and joints that you are most able to glimpse what lies beneath.

In philosophy, too, it is the linkings and the meshings that are most instructive, as when life seems to emanate from matter or humanity from the animalism of the big apes. The most urgent things for you to know lie hidden at the point of origin.

Has it ever occurred to you how much a person could learn from one single experience that would be repeated again and again but in different ways throughout a lifetime? Very likely this idea lies behind the familiar expression "by thinking about it all the time."

Look at those painters who have constantly dealt with the same theme, painted the same face or the same tree, and who in that one thing, offered so abundantly, never despaired of reaching the universal.

The flair of genius consists in detecting and keeping an eye on particular things that contain a potential universal and which through accumulated analogies can greatly enlarge our knowledge. If you study Pascal's method of working, the most amazing thing about it is his ability to choose those instances in which "nature imitates herself," or from which you can draw numerous properties that are useful in other areas, as well as so many things from the human realm, like amusement, contradiction, the fickleness of justice, and so on. Choose a seam or a site or a situation; seed it with doubts and endless questions; explore it thoroughly; combine its unique qualities with its shared resemblances to give it the dimensions of a total thing: this is the foundation of culture, at least of culture as man, in his short existence, can hope to encompass it.

Culture does not consist in skimming over the whole body of knowledge or of entrenching yourself in a specialization but in digging right where you are until you break through into the drift your neighbor has dug, and then in seeing where and how all your efforts converge. This demands a common spirit and aspiration, and it presupposes a common language.

You may imagine a circle. Then suppose that an intelligent and most conscientious creature has landed from somewhere on its rim, and that he assigns himself the task of learning what this shape is on which he has happened. You can call this creature A. One possible method would be for A to travel around the whole length of the circumference, step by step. This is the encyclopedic method, the method you are likely to choose first, because human beings are greedy to "find out," and they hugely enjoy going forward without going beneath the surface—a passion that twelve years in school foster in you. But $A$ can travel the whole way around his circle without ever realizing that he now resides in a circle and that a circle is what he is circumventing. At this point, you may allow $A$ a little intuition and application; endow him with the ability to make an effort and to persevere in it. Now $A$ will choose a point somewhere along the circumference; he will strike off from that toward the center; he will follow one line, moving in the direction of the point from which all lines radiate; he will reach (and do give him every break) the center $O$. From then on, he will understand that he landed on a circle, and he can even have the satisfaction of being able to produce the circle. This illustrates two ways of learning: the one, the way of temptation, sends you scurrying over the surface in endless agitation, and disorients you by making you believe that everything is different from everything else; the other, on the contrary, leads you back to the circle and makes you realize with serene delight what resemblances the varied elements of experience possess among them.

# 4

# The Monster

# and His Rest

The effort here discussed cannot be sustained. One characteristic of all human labor is that it is necessarily imperfect. In big things as in small, activity gives way to relaxation. Start, stop; start, stop. These twin actions would be very hard to manage if nature did not step in and undertake to furnish you with the desire to act, then with fatigue, and then oblivion.

It is a serious misunderstanding of the mind's nature to think of it only in terms of activity.

Were you more attentive to yourselves, if you knew how to observe yourselves in all phases of living, you would be amazed at the long stretches of time that seem like blanks, useless zones, small abysses in the center of consciousness. Night brings clarification; the mind disciplines itself and matures simply with the passing of time. The great boon of sleep is to avoid disproportion.

Any work demands that you concentrate on one point. It is not necessarily the main point, however. It would be a very good thing if you were to move quickly on. Every stroke of the pick takes you farther from the cen-

ter, dulls your hearing, and showers you with dust and
debris. Every act of close attention contracts the mind;
it demands that you momentarily forget everything that
is not immediate and urgent; it makes you tense, and
upsets a certain balance. Of course, you must not scorn
attentive minds, even if the object of their attention is
insignificant. Any and all precision represents a victory.
But you must remember that to focus your attention on
one detail, if you are not at the same time mindful of
the whole, involves a risk, and being aware of the whole
is akin to resting because it requires a relaxing of the
intelligence and even of the will. Napoleon was able
to fall asleep whenever he wished; as he said, he closed
all his drawers. He claimed that it is useful to be able
to sleep during battle. When all dispositions have been
taken, the orders all issued, and the outcome cannot yet
be foreseen, there is always the risk that one be misled
or panicked by some isolated, partial development.
Sleep soothes any nervousness; it leaves your strength
intact and your mind clear. After a period of relaxation,
you are more effectively tensed for action. This is why
Descartes made it a rule never to work except when he
had had a long rest and had his full resources well in
hand.

Rest bears another fruit; it ripens. Many contemporary books lack what might be called the third dimen-
sion. The ideas they offer are flat and seem to be painted
on the surface of the mind; they have not been set forth
in the context of time, which would have provided perspective and relief. "When we are young," Goethe once
said to Eckermann, "we see things from a single point
of view, whereas a great work demands a plurality of
views, and there's where we come to grief." This explains Goethe's habit of keeping his manuscripts for
such a long time; he set them aside, took them up
again, and put them in final form as late as possible,

when his own life would have passed over into them. You must keep telling yourselves that in your work every retard—assuming that the work is soundly launched— represents one more "chance to reap ripe fruit." One bitter day Sainte-Beuve wrote in his diary: "To ripen, O, to ripen! One grows tough here, rotten there, but one does not ripen." It's all too true that it is hard to carry a thought, a project, a feeling through to that degree of unfolded development which is maturity. Time paves the way for the completion of work; it strips away nonessentials, sloughs off the accidental. And again it acts positively in causing to sprout what once was only a seed.

## II

I believe that one rule for the good workman is that he know how to separate the phases of his work. I've already talked about the advantages of not letting periods of leisure and application overlap, for this mixture produces a bastard kind of half-work; we French spend hours toiling away at our desk and get nowhere near the results the phlegmatic Anglo-Saxon does. This, then, is sound advice; insofar as possible, divide intellectual work into three periods: the time to make the monsters; the time to rest; the time to complete—that is, to perfect—the work. This chapter will deal with the first two phases.

The word "monster" I have borrowed from Maurice Barrès (1862-1923), whose novels in the early twentieth century won a tremendous popularity. Barrès' fellow writer, J. Tharaud, described the methods Barrès used to produce his admirable prose. The best thing I can do here is to quote directly:

"In Barrès' study, where I spent so much time, I had

an experience few writers have known. It is quite usual for painters to work in the studio of some established artist. There the student learns his calling—methods and rules that he can think about in relation to his own work and that he is free to accept or reject. There is no such training for writers. The painter's art—the sculptor's, too—has an element of technique that appears to have no equivalent in writing. But this only seems to be so. Literature also has techniques and methods, which it is useful to know, and one either learns them from others or loses endless time learning them by oneself—or risks never knowing them. Yet chance rarely puts a young writer in a position where, as happened to me, he can observe a great writer at work. Ordinarily, the writer loves solitude; he cannot endure a strange presence around him. On the other hand, the aspiring young writer is quick to imagine that he will lose his talent by learning from others. I do believe this is a mistaken notion; genuine originality develops in response to cultivation and not in response to a void; if the talent is real, it can only be helped to discover itself through such commerce.

"For me Barrès' study was like a studio. He did not teach me what cannot be taught—self-discovery, invention, all that comes to one from the unconscious—but he did teach me how one creates for oneself the most favorable conditions in which to organize a work of art. When I first went to him, I had that absurd notion that the masterpiece springs forth suddenly and miraculously from the mind. I believed in inspiration alone. Actually, this is a most sterilizing idea; nothing fosters laziness more. You constantly put off working; you wait for heaven knows what spirit of grace and illumination to descend; you can never believe that you are quite in the right condition and frame of mind to work. Time passes and you do nothing.

"I had another idea, too, no less idiotic, that you could not progress with your task if you left any loose ends—that is, if you left any part of it unfinished or incomplete. Now, my feeble talent was not equal to bringing forth only perfect chapters first time round, and I would become impatient and my efforts landed in the wastebasket. I kept going over and over and over the same ground. Instead of looking toward the road ahead, I was forever looking backward. I had no feeling of ease or freedom, only a precarious relief that I had got something written down and a kind of terror at the prospect of what I had still to do. In short, I lived in a state of feverish strain and a constant reaching for I don't know what absolute standard, which resulted sometimes in disgust and a heap of crumpled waste-paper, sometimes in a stiff, lifeless revision, and sometimes in flashes that seemed to me inspired at one moment and nothing but empty bombast the next.

"The great, the incalculable thing that Barrès taught me was how to be modest about my work. I can never thank him enough. Not that I immediately recognized his helpfulness. At first, I was scandalized, and it was only with practice that my ideas changed radically.

"He did not believe in the masterpiece that springs full-blown from the head of Zeus. His initial approach to a subject was so humble that I found it upsetting. He could see no beginning, middle, or end. He had before him only a vast, inchoate mass of material, dimly outlined through a kind of fog. He snatched this or that detail as it emerged from the shadows. Often just a brief clue, a word, a hasty sign, a flash of intuition rather than a thought, but it sufficed to mark a spot where something further was to be looked for; now and then precise indications; from time to time—the way it happens when you are out hunting—a snapped twig that marks the trail and guarantees your finding your way back. All these things were grouped together according to some vague affinities; like coats of many colors, they were filled out little by little with the substance of his meditations.

"For him these fruitful moments came at night— during periods of insomnia (he knew them well) or in those critical hours when the weary mind drifts aimlessly or skirts an apocalyptic nightmare, yet at the same time is hovering near some fresh thought, never before perceived, that emerges barefoot from the shadows. Barrès never allowed that moment to escape him and to slip into nothingness but snatched it as it passed. He would take up the paper and pencil that he put every evening on a table by his bed, and in the dark, in a scrawl that he could scarcely decipher next morning, he would jot down phrases that were still bathed in the mystery of sleep and that the light of day would have frightened away. . . . Or again, he might be listening to some palaver in Parliament when an idea would suddenly spurt from a private reverie he had not checked together with his overcoat in the cloakroom, and this he would scribble on a scrap of paper or the back of an envelope. . . . Or he might fetch back a nugget from the long walks we used to take together in Paris. Many times we would have strolled on for two or three hours, talking about everything under the sun, for he liked to talk as he walked. Back in his study, before getting down to work, he almost always took one of his notebooks—or a sheet of loose paper if the material concerned current work—and noted a sequence of impressions or ideas that had taken shape in his mind. Almost always what he recorded was completely foreign to the conversation we had had. Things had slipped secretly between us without my realizing it, until I saw him jotting them down as we sat facing each other across his worktable. Once I expressed my astonishment, and he said to me, 'Well, you see, that is my gift.'

"A whole part of his work, the mysterious part, was done in this way—outside his study, and without his will's intervening except to orient his mind in a certain direction, the way we, by falling asleep with a given idea in mind, impose a dream upon the night. 'I don't make things,' he used to say. 'Things make themselves inside me.' All these windfalls, whether from the unconscious or the waking mind, were woven together in cloaks of many colors. Everything was caught up and stored away, nothing that passed through his mind was allowed to slip away. These scattered fragments—of very uneven quality, brilliant ones making others seem thin and flat—comprised in the end a substantial, albeit shapeless, mass to which he gave a marvelously appropriate name. He called it his 'monster.'

" 'A monster! But a monster that exists. A shaggy realty, but one you can lean on.' "

Let me keep Barrès' word "monster," privately mindful of another monster born of genius—Pascal's "Pensées." What are "The Meditations," after all, if not a jumble of things that should have appeared in all their perfection in a finished masterpiece that never came to be? Pascal prepared his groundwork with care; he used to note down whatever came to mind—a quotation, an unfinished train of thought, a word, a phrase that had come to him spontaneously and that he was eager to preserve for the chance sparkle you can never recapture. His notebook was a kind of angler's creel into which he tossed more or less finished fragments; he also stored away ideas about order and arrangement that he was not yet ready to choose among for fear the work would take shape and harden too quickly. Pascal also left in his monster the notes from his reading and other references. Nor, like any good workman, did he neglect to throw in reflections about the art of writing and to describe his own work experiences. And much as the farmer grunts and groans behind his plow, the groan being almost essential to a good furrow, so Pascal recorded his own prayers and laments—the "humiliations through which he offered himself up to inspiration." Everything imaginable is to be found in this topsy-turvy melange of life that moves onward through crisis after crisis. Pascal did not realize that in this way he was adding more to French language and thought than he possibly could have with a work pushed through to formal completion, and that these fragments would be better calculated to teach than would an outwardly perfect work.

For our purposes, you might retain from all this one peerless precept: the "monster" is the result of your forcing yourselves to write the thing down the moment it has happened, for better or for worse, unhesitatingly, irrevocably.

You must exercise some self-control, obviously. You have to see ahead, anticipate, go beyond what you think you know or can do. Most of the time you don't realize your own capacities; you know more than you think you know. A monster is delivered in travail.

But there is a world of difference between the poorest rough draft and the purest idea that is left unexpressed. The monster will be your original clay. You would not believe what an advantage it is to have this initial resistant material to which you can apply yourself. It is easier to correct or to rub out or to begin again than it is to invent or create. *The most deplorable sentence is better than a blank sheet of paper.* Balzac knew this work law. Waiting for inspiration is a futile exercise. The thing to do is to pick up your raw material and get your hands dirty. Alain quotes this advice from Stendhal: "As late as 1806, I was waiting for genius to descend upon me so that I might write. . . . If I had spoken around 1795 of my plan to write, some sensible man would have told me, 'Write every day for an hour or two.' Genius or no genius. That advice would have made me use ten years of my life that I spent stupidly waiting for genius."

## III

Must the monster always appear as a scribble? I had a friend who would never have had the audacity to shake off his laziness about writing if he had not let himself be tempted by a well-sharpened pencil, a sheet of white paper, and if he had not set casually about his work. He had his article published in a modest, even obscure magazine. As he put it, in this way he enjoyed "the satisfaction of seeing myself published without the fear of being read." He had played a game with himself, realizing that the desire for perfection freezes us and that we are sterilized by the specter of excellence.

But there is sometimes an advantage in giving birth to your monster in broad daylight, and I'd like now to own up to a device that has occasionally helped me when I cannot get started. I obtain a notebook of particularly good quality paper; I take pains to make it look attractive, a little bit as if I were illuminating a missal; ignoring the smiles around me, I sometimes go so far as to cover the pages with a light blue or mauve wash, or with that shade of yellow belonging to old walls and old faces. Then I lay down one rule for myself—to write on this parchment without erasing, as if I were copying a finished piece from memory. Why is the mind helped by this paradoxical method? Because now your concentration is put on its mettle. You know you will not be revising, so you decide in cold blood to have no regrets and to correct the past not by going over it but by beginning again: let the dead bury the dead. It was Victor Hugo who said that the best way to correct a book is to write a second that may be better. The same principle can apply to a sentence. Try this method; if you use it regularly, you will understand the method of a Montaigne, a Saint-Simon, or more recently, a Péguy, Alain, or Claudel—in other words, the method followed by writers who are always active, who let their pen run on, entrusting themselves to it as they would to a stallion whose kicking and shying they forgive provided the creature has spirit.

This advice cannot be urged on everybody, yet it is good to force yourself sometimes to be perfect. "Excellence," Henri Rambaud said, "costs less trouble than mediocrity."

I have thought now and then that these two methods of producing a draft manuscript correspond to two methods of the sculptor. Following the first, he works and shapes his clay. The writer's equivalent approach is to enter into contact with language, then to feel his way, the way the sculptor's hand struggles with the earth that simultaneously resists and guides him. The second is the method of the sculptor who attacks a block of marble and hews a shape from it. In this case, he is not beginning with a material that changes at his touch but one that every instant risks being transformed and spoiled. He has before him a hard, inviolable material, one that allows no retouching. When you work with marble, you must think that the figure exists already and that your task is not so much to invent as to discover and release that figure, veil by veil, as if it were drowsing within the stone. Perhaps that is why Michelangelo has left us so many sleeping figures.

IV

Once the monster is born, it's advisable to imitate the sower of seeds—disappear, that is, and make room for the silent co-operator in our first efforts to do his part. I mean time.

There is a relationship between composition and time; it is time working within us that composes. Gide has some valuable things to say about this in his "Journal": "I consider the composition of a book of primary importance, and I think that most books today suffer from not having been composed. The essence of what I mean is this: it is best to let the work compose and order itself —above all else, not to force it. I am using the word 'force' in the horticultural sense: forced growth is a method of cultivation that brings plants to a premature flowering. I think that the major flaw of artists and writers today is impatience; if they knew how to wait, their subject would slowly compose itself in their minds; it would free itself of underbrush and grow as a tree grows. . . . It is through composition that an artist gives depth to his canvas. Without composition the work of art could present only a superficial beauty. . . ."

Work is actually being accomplished in this interval, which only seems to be empty. The mind is host to speculations, preoccupations, a concern for possible gaps and omissions, plans in a process of evolving—"dynamic," Bergson called them. The mind teems with questions of how to proceed, which road to follow, with perspectives to choose. The mind never sleeps. "I sleep," the Spouse said, "but my heart waketh" (Song of Sol. 5-2). Is it not true that a mother does not sleep a deep sleep, since a child's sigh awakens her? This state of half-wakeful-ness, half-sleep, is the repose I am speaking of; it is a kind of patient availability.

A typical activity when I am in this state of mind is to set up a series of index cards, which I number one, two, three, four, and so on, in the upper right-hand corner, and arrange in a file box. Each number is connected with a single axial thought. Everything related to this idea—notes, drafts, magazine or newspaper clips —will be filed under the appropriate card. This is a very relaxed operation, for you are in a period of rest when the mind should remain receptive, vacant, and inattentive.

Each and every particle of dust has its value when swept up by the whirlwind. Leibniz rejected almost nothing. What enabled him to find a place for so much was the fact that, like a luminous wheel, a multitude of rays issued from his mind like so many spokes; these rays were the latent directions and the suspended action —I call it waiting—that are the soul of attention.

Poverty dwells in the mind and not in the things without. If you had Ideas, how many things you would see!

Each axis of thought is a promise and a hope, and chances are infinite in number. Every time two independent series cross one another, a fresh chance is created—or so it is said. If you accept this, then you will see that chance is really constant, since you yourselves are one of these series and the outside world is the other. Your inner life flows on without reference to the universe. The people who speak with you know nothing of your desires or your past or how that past now crops out; they are unaware of everything you are. And yet it happens that a gesture or word or action of theirs assumes a meaning in this inner context that concerns you alone. It is the same with the life of the mind. When you have some questions boldly put, some work plan or project sketched out, then events, conversation, reading (even reading of material that does not bear directly on the subject that interests you)—everything brings nourishment and may even supply the solution to your problem.

Once the lines of thought have been laid down, you can slip serenely into that half-sleeping, half-waking state in which the mind is poised to welcome the slightest stirring of thought.

# 5

# Putting Your
# Thoughts in Order

The time finally comes when you must produce. It is
a painful moment. Few people would endure it if they
were not forced to. It's lucky that Balzac was head over
heels in debt; otherwise, his material would have dozed
away inside him instead of being transformed into
novels. If you were not made to bring your inner impulses out into the open, you would never give them
expression. It is such an agony to give body to thought.

So it is good for you to be pressured by some obliga-
tion and a deadline. It is even useful to have too little
time. Students are better off than they think when they
must work against the clock on a class-written composition. As the clock strikes and reminds you that the
hour is drawing to its inexorable end, those of you who
do not let yourselves be rattled are actually stimulated.
In ordinary life, it is often hard to set up such time limits
for yourselves, especially since you never quite know
when a work of the mind is finished. "I do not know of
any finished work," Valéry said once. "I know only of
abandoned work." Still, the moment must come when
the uncertain fruit is plucked from the tree. The editor

who wrenched the manuscript of "Le cimetiere marin" from Valéry (who was complaining to friends that the work was not maturing), like the other publisher who snatched the manuscript of "Les deux sources" from Bergson, performed services to literature and to their victims as well.


I


Now see if you can advance the monster from draft to coherent order—a problem that Pascal had the wit to sidestep by dying at the right moment. However, only a universal genius of demonstrated heroism and saintliness like his can endow a draft with lasting value. It behooves the rest of you to complete your work, and this can be done only by the taxing process of weighing, calculating and arranging.

By all means, remind yourselves at the outset that there is no perfect order. Whatever the organization of the material, you might always prefer another arrangement and find reasonable arguments to justify that choice. The thing here is not to let yourselves be distracted by the idea of "the most perfect" plan but to develop as lucidly as possible the one that has occurred to you.

To this end, reread your notes and see which relate to the same subject. Thought is musical; it presupposes themes that disappear and reappear. But how are you to recognize your own themes?

You will arrange your notes in groups, the way Pascal's editors did with his notes. When you have done this, you will have created clusters of ideas.

I will assume that with this step you will have detected your basic themes. The next step is to arrange them in a given order.

Order is the royal highway that leads from the simple to the complex, from the known to the unknown, from what is granted by everyone to what is perceived only by the most perspicacious intelligences.

There is a device for testing whether the various parts of a composition are well arranged. It is simply to ask yourself if you can conclude each section with the formula, "There is more to come." If I were teaching composition or rhetoric, this is the Open Sesame that I would offer my young students at the very beginning.

More remains to be done, however. I know that today most people do not observe the rule I am going to give, although, until recently, it was as ineluctable as good manners. People do not trouble to put order into their writing; they pass their conglomerations directly on to the reader. Authors deliver to their publishers manuscripts which are like crude ore; the mere absence of judiciously spaced indentations—paragraphs—is a clue to the reader that he need not look for any links between ideas. Or, on the other hand, the author may deliver his work in fragments, neglecting transitions, as if he were publishing random posthumous notes.

Now, it is true that talent stands above rules, indeed, stands revealed when it has freed itself from them. "O grammarian," Claudel said, "in my poems do not seek the pathway, seek the center." Yet we teachers may be permitted to prefer the old methods, which counseled us to refine our writing (the old expression was "to chasten"); that is, to prune everything that is not essential but at the same time to express everything that is indispensable. The writer's task in former days was not construed as one of reproducing his private, inner monologue or of making oracular pronouncements; he was expected to stop midway between the flood of an unparagraphed page and the jerky discontinuity of the aphorism.

## II

Sometimes a teacher has occasion to ask himself why a student's paper, excellent as it is, bears some mark of immaturity. Nothing has been omitted; he can single out passages that would do credit to a professional writer. What, then, is lacking? What is the difference between what the human mind can produce on the same subject at fifty or at sixteen?

Young students emphatically do not lack talent, even genius. Their difficulty is that they have too many ideas, and they do not know how to choose one and develop that. It is as if nature got the notion of creating a tree that is at once beech, oak, and birch, and simply could not resign herself to the existence of different species.

Superabundance is a frequent flaw in books; everything is said, nothing stands out in relief. In a period like ours, which finds the virtue of maturity in the feverishly confused outpourings of adolescence, young people can be excused. And some literary sagas do command admiration; it certainly requires more skill to sustain and direct a three-thousand-page novel than to chisel a sonnet sequence; "Les Misérables" is a more remarkable achievement than "Trophées." Note, however, that you sometimes choose the supersize work, despite all its pitfalls, because you sense your inability to control your work; that is, really to compose it, to concentrate and to choose. You hand everything over to the reader, wine and dregs together.

So a teacher should not necessarily advise young people to amass ideas or information, or to pile sentence upon sentence, but, on the contrary, to select one idea and to display it, like a length of fine fabric, so as to show its full texture, color, and drape. Once upon a time, rhetoric taught students how to do this. Considerable pedantry and obscurity were involved, no doubt, but was the approach basically mistaken?

The new rhetoric should be stripped of the superfluous, just as Descartes long ago purified logic and algebra and reduced them to a few principles. He said, and he was right, that a multitude of rules is an excuse for laziness. The human mind is clever, always quick to find excuses. It will adopt the most stringent rules and make the most heroic resolutions precisely in order to escape having to follow them, saying secretly, "These rules are too much for me. Nobody could follow them." If you want to make progress in your life and work, you must make a hard decision; you must settle on a simple rule that you can practice daily, and then keep at it for several months. It was to this end that I looked for an exercise that students could readily do and that at the same time would yield rich results.

By a stroke of good luck, when I was sixteen I admired a book called "Literary Method," that had as subtitle, "Diary of a High School Teacher." The author was a man by the name of Bézard, who used to teach in the Lycée Hoche in Versailles. I don't know whether the book is still in print, but I would give a lot to find a copy and rediscover many useful things I know I've forgotten. The book brought you right into the middle of a high-school classroom; it was rather like lifting the roof of a hive and watching the bees busily making their honey. M. Bézard never stated a rule without immediately giving an example of how it worked—giving even poor or mistaken examples, too, for he included among other things some of his own students' ideas and work. Many textbooks are spoiled, in my opinion, because they confront you only with perfect examples; as models, these are too far beyond your reach to be helpful.

Another thing that Bézard taught was how to take

notes and how to set up card files that are useful a whole lifetime. If I had followed his advice, today I would have a gold mine; none of my early work would have been lost. What is so discouraging about studying is to see that knowledge is never solidly possessed, that it does not remain with you, does not constantly grow and expand, as you half assume it must. If only I had known this isn't true! If only I had followed Bézard's advice about taking notes. The few times I did, I have been rewarded; thirty years later, cards that I prepared according to his directions are still useful to me.

Bézard taught, fair weather or foul, the theory of the paragraph. He had borrowed it from the great teachers of the past—Taine, Prévost-Paradol, Brunetière. The theory of the paragraph is the law of all composition. Of course, you can ignore it, and you *should* ignore it as you progress and as school fades as an influence in life. You must renounce the rules in all things if you want to achieve the full savor of your art. But you must have mastered those rules in order to bypass them.

I am speaking now for the benefit of beginners, and proposing exercises analogous to musical scales, or closed ranks in military drill, or spoken prayers—the exercises which you see champions reverting to if they want to keep in condition.

The doctrine of the paragraph, if you really understand it, supplies you with the means for writing well, for setting forth your ideas effectively, just as the practice of taking notes helps you to read well and to derive a long-term profit from your reading. The greatest service that can be rendered a young student is teaching him this work method.

It is founded on a clear and certain principle—but one that you quickly forget the moment you start expounding your views: it is the narrow, wavering nature of human attention. Attention is like a slender-necked bottle, and precious elixir must be poured into it drop by drop. The mind is flighty; attention is like a lighthouse beacon that flashes on, off, and on again. Possibly this is connected with the in-and-out movement of breathing. Therefore, to make yourselves understood you must not so much compose as *dis*compose—that is, insofar as possible, say one thing at a time. What is more, you must repeat. A teacher of foreign languages told me once that he felt his students had really learned a word when they had forgotten and relearned it nine times. To be able to express a thought clearly, you must first dissect it and observe not only all the facets that comprise its subject but also the underlying elements implicit in it. Once you know these facets and basic principles, you set them forth, one by one. It's a good idea to watch someone sew while you are working. It reminds you that everything, in life as in work, is done one stitch at a time.

Whether you are teaching or writing or propagandizing, the problem is to repeat yourself without giving the impression that you are doing so. The ear and the mind like to find again, in a new guise, something that they have just perceived (this is the appeal of rhyme), but they just as heartily dislike having the same thing repeated in the same way. In private conversations, General Foch confessed that in war the art of command consisted in maintaining against wind and tide the same order while changing the tune, so that the troops would always have the impression of something new, without which their morale quickly collapsed. You have to find new and different ideas to circumvent the tedium of fighting and dying. Goethe had similar ideas, and so did Bergson. Repeat, but with a difference; say the same thing, but in a fresh way—this is the perennial rule for communicating with human beings. The order of love, Pascal said mysteriously, the order without semblance of order that he admired in the Evangelists, consists in digressing from a point, which is reintroduced later so that it is always kept present.

Taking off from here, I used to tell my students that the art of expression consisted in saying the same thing three times. You state the given idea; you develop it; you recapitulate it briefly. Then you move on to another idea. Some of my early students turned this prescription into a ditty:

> You say that you are going to say it;
> Then you say it;
> Then you say that you've said it.

I used to let them chant this, tapping out the beat, and I remember that once the headmaster came by and did a real double-take to hear thirty resonant young voices chorusing "You say that you've said it." All the same, it was a useful rule—as effective as it was rarely followed.

I was so convinced of this—sensing that thought is truly gaited to move backward, that art consists in transforming intuitions into conclusions, and that the last thing to be discovered is the initial, prompting idea —that I used to teach my young people to make the first sentence they wrote on a fresh white page appear down at the bottom as their concluding sentence. Words to this effect: "Thus it is that. . . ."

This process of reversing the natural work of the mind—of starting off from the end you wish to reach and going back to first principles—is the method Edgar Allan Poe says he followed, and he recommends it in his essay, "The Philosophy of Composition." He recalls that, in a letter, Dickens refers to the fact that "Godwin wrote his 'Caleb Williams' backwards. He first involved his hero in a web of difficulties, forming the second volume, and then, for the first, cast about him for some mode of accounting for what had been done." Poe goes on to remark that "every plot worth the name must be elaborated to its denouement before anything be attempted with the pen."

## III

The passage in which Poe relates how he composed "The Raven" is highly instructive. He was unusually aware of methods, and approached the writing of poetry with a concern akin to that of a mechanical engineer. His objective was to create a certain *effect* on the reader. With this in mind, Poe asked himself what would be the preferable symbol. Having decided that as symbol the raven best answered the purpose of his poem, he then determined the number of lines that such a piece should have in order to produce the most intense poetic impression. He selected the rhythm most likely to create it. But he particularly sought for a refrain, which should occur again and again and be, as it were, the musical key to the composition. It should be, he decided, a single word that had a profound and melancholy meaning, that was agreeably sonorous, short enough to be recognized and retained, long enough and attenuated enough to persist in memory like a mournful echo. All these reasons led him to the long "o" as the most sonorous vowel together with "r" as the most producible consonant—a long-drawn, languourous sound preceded by relatively flat-sounding syllables; and he finally chose the word "nevermore."

## IV

Now perhaps I will be forgiven if I quote the passage that I dictate to new students early in the school term. Not right at the beginning; a lesson is profitable when the victim has known some keenly felt failures and come to realize where he is weak; only after he has fallen three times has he the right to a lesson in how to walk.

"As a house is built of bricks, an essay is composed of paragraphs.

"A paragraph is the space between two indentations. A paragraph should have from fifteen to twenty-five lines.

"Where is the *head* of the paragraph to be found, that is to say, the directing, propelling part? At the *tail* end. The conclusion of the paragraph expresses its intent, and that is why we finish a paragraph with a sentence that summarizes its meaning.

"This suggests a good way of learning how to write a good paragraph. It is to take a sheet of blank paper and about three lines up from the bottom to write 'It is in this way that.' . . . Or other phrases, such as: 'One sees, therefore' . . . , 'Let us say that' . . . , 'In conclusion' . . . , 'Therefore' . . . , 'One can therefore say that' . . . , 'Finally' . . . , 'In short' . . . , 'Let us recapitulate' . . . , 'No one will deny that' . . . , 'It will be agreed that.' Such a formula will elicit the conclusion of the paragraph—a striking, lapidary sentence that is simple, clear, even abrupt, often paradoxical. We construct the rest of the paragraph in function of this sentence.

"The introductory sentence links such a concluding phrase with what is to follow: 'We have seen that' . . . , 'Let us see whether.' . . .

"And now I am going to dictate to you a typical paragraph, quoted from Bergson's 'Laughter':

" 'The first point to which attention should be called is that the comic does not exist outside the pale of what is strictly *human*. A landscape may be beautiful, charming and sublime, or insignificant and ugly; it will never be laughable. You may laugh at an animal, but only because you have detected in it some human attitude or expression. You may laugh at a hat, but what you are making fun of, in this case, is not the piece of felt or straw, but the shape that men have given it—the human caprice whose mould it has assumed. It is strange that so important a fact, and such a simple one, too, has not attracted to a greater degree the attention of philosophers. Several have defined man as "an animal which laughs." They might equally well have defined him as an animal which is laughed at; for if any other animal, or some lifeless object, produces the same effect, it is always because of some resemblance to man, of the stamp he gives it or the use he puts it to.

" 'Here I would point out, as a symptom equally worthy of notice, the *absence of feeling* which usually accompanies laughter. [Bergson goes on to develop this idea more fully and concludes:] To produce the whole of its effect, then, the comic demands something like a momentary anesthesia of the heart. Its appeal is to intelligence, pure and simple.'[1]

"How do *you* build a paragraph? How do you make ideas spring from barren soil? That is what we will tell you now.

"There are three methods by which to develop an idea: 1) *a priori;* 2) *a posteriori;* 3) *a contrario.*

"As an experiment, let us take the proposition, 'Wealth does not make for happiness.'

"The first—the *a priori* method—is this: you deduce the proposition you want to establish from more general propositions which everyone accepts as true and from which yours follows as a matter of course.

"For example: an individual's well-being cannot be

[1] From "Laughter," by Henri Bergson, which is contained in *Comedy* copyright © 1956 by Wylie Sypher. Reprinted by permission of Doubleday & Company, Inc.

found in any thing foreign to the nature of man, therefore. . . .

"Happiness is a psychic state of being that results
from an idea. It is, therefore, not wealth but the idea
of wealth that creates happiness. . . .

"*A priori* reasoning is difficult because the choice of
the first principle is a delicate one. Moreover, it has
primarily a logical value. *A posteriori* reasoning is much
easier.

"The *a posteriori* method consists in taking examples,
facts, concrete cases from real life, anecdotes, and so
on that bear out your contention.

"By way of example: the case of Croesus.

"You should note, by the way, that it is not the quantity but the quality of your examples that will make your
point. Small minds operate on the basis of quantity.
Great minds operate on the basis of quality and depth.
They choose one significant example from among all
those available and examine it thoroughly. Once you
have analyzed a typical fact, however, it is a good idea
to show that you are familiar with others, too. This is
what we call 'allusion.' In making use of allusion, you
husband your knowledge, display your intelligence agreeably, and broaden the perspective on the subject in question. (Also, allusion is always flattering to your reader.)

"To reason in this way—on the basis of facts—requires an effort of memory and of analysis. It will always hold a reader's interest. It does not, however,
involve the reader's feelings. In this respect, reasoning
*a contrario* is quite different.

"The *a contrario* method is this: you introduce an
objection, develop it vigorously, and then ascertain,

a) what part of truth there may be in it, and
whether it is a seeming or secondary truth;

b) what part of error there may be.

"For example: *Shall one say that* wealth gives man

the means of satisfying all his desires and of being therefore happy?

"*Beyond doubt,* wealth does allow a man to satisfy his
material and even his aesthetic needs . . .

". . . *but* wealth cannot satisfy the essential needs of
a man's mind or spirit.

"*Shall one say, then, that* the rich man has, thanks
to his fortune, the means of increasing his generosity?

"*Beyond doubt,* the wealth of an unselfish man en-
ables him to increase his generosity tenfold . . .

". . . *but* in this instance it is not his wealth but his
virtue that gives him happiness. In other words, wealth
augments his *acts* of generosity but not his generosity
itself.

"*A contrario* is both more appealing to the reader
and more productive for the author. It engages the fine
edge of the mind and helps it trace that delicate line
that separates what seems to us true from what seems
to us false. It even allows us to bring out what in the
false is true—I mean, the element of truth that to our
way of thinking is to be found in our opponent's idea.

"Do not imagine that you must apply these three
methods to every paragraph you write. They are like a
necessary scaffolding—the structure of argument that
we must always have in mind and always forget."

## V

If this theory of the paragraph is to be really profitable, it must rest on the collateral theory of note-taking,
which will be discussed more fully in the next chapter.
Here let me simply say that one of the best things in
Bézard was that he taught both at once—how to write
paragraphs and how to take notes. A pleasant economy,
when the same principle serves two purposes.

A useful note taken in the course of your reading should be a paragraph in outline. Like a paragraph, a note should contain only one idea. This time the idea should be set forth at the top rather than at the bottom of your page. It should be disjointed or divided into two or three adjacent ideas, or supported by one or two examples, and, if possible, enlivened with an illustration or so of how it can be applied. Reading then becomes the act of extracting from a book five or six notes organized around several central ideas.

This method of summarizing what you have read has many advantages. It obliges a youthful mind to search out essentials, and to develop the ability to cope with general ideas—I mean not abstract but general ideas, ideas that are based on actual texts or facts and that can, additionally, bring light to bear on other facts, known or unknown. This method represents a return to the mind's natural way of functioning. And you end up by having in your possession a little stock of possible paragraphs that can be used in various compositions or speeches—a kind of strategic reserve that you can throw into the breach to shore up a crumbling position in any future battle.

The *organized note* and the *organizing paragraph* sustain and complement each other. The first teaches you how to make one thing out of multiple things: it teaches you to summarize. The second teaches you how to make multiple things out of a single thing: it teaches you to develop. To summarize and to develop are two phases of the same operation, as inhaling and exhaling are two moments in living.

Beginners should be trained to carry out these two operations together, according to some advice that Taine gave his nephew Chevrillon: "I'll tell you the method I've found most useful in writing," he said, "and even more so in rewriting or revising a draft that is perhaps too densely written or too loosely constructed. I make an analytical summary of the contents of each chapter. This is the brief listing that appears (in small or italic type) at the head of a chapter. I prepare this not when I am beginning or have finished, but as I am going along, after each paragraph. It is just one line, and is the most accurate, precise summation of the paragraph that I can make. I have to try several times before I find the phrase, but once it's found, it shows me what is overwritten and must be pruned, what gaps must be filled in, what lapses from logic and clarity and order need to be remedied, for everything in the paragraph must lead toward the summary. Furthermore, this summary suggests possible summaries for the next paragraph, and taken all together, they suggest the essence of your next chapter."

It is worth repeating: the value of a summary is not so much a matter of giving the substance of what you have already thought as of orienting you toward what you are going to think. The good summary is a prospector's tool.

## VI

"What I like is reworking my work," Valéry said. "Beginnings I find tedious and anything that comes to me right off I always suspect can be improved. The spontaneous thing, even if excellent, even if captivating, never seems to me to be sufficiently my own."

It is true, the search for perfection through revision is a pleasure. Yet it can happen that your vision becomes weary and clouded; by tampering with your colors, you can muddy them. The real way to correct work is to sleep on it and to begin afresh—the way, in Homer, the warriors lie down upon their couches in the evening and rise refreshed to greet the rosy-fingered dawn.

And then you must remind yourself that in man perfection comes from contrast; the poor is essential to the good, the body of the lyre to its strings—and that you must, after all, allow criticism its role. After the French critic Albert Thibaudet died, Bergson wrote: "When a book of two hundred pages contains ten that are instructive or stimulating, we should thank the author and act as if the rest had not been written. The best among us know well enough that what are judged our finest ideas have been culled from among others that were less so or that were not so at all. . . . Such authors have simply had the good sense to keep what was good. Their superiority has been to detect their own mediocrity, when they were being mediocre, in time."

Be quiet when you have nothing worthwhile to say—this advice applies to young and old alike. The silence of the man who refrains from speaking is an instructive and resounding silence.

# 6

# Reading

# As Self-Enrichment

"Subdue your thirst for books," Marcus Aurelius said, "so that you may die not babbling but at peace."

It is astonishing what lip service people pay to conventional standards when they talk about their own reading.

To hear them, they have read every book that happens to be mentioned: the classics (that goes without saying), all the new prize-winners, all the outstanding foreign books. Yet a simple calculation shows that people's reading capacity is limited, except in the case of professional critics who can assess a book's content by flipping through it. Subtract from the ordinary man's life the time given over to work, worries, routine physical care, social contacts, getting about from place to place, accidents, and so on, and you see how very little is left for reading. The man who has read ten books a year for fifty years will have learned only an infinitesimal part of what the smallest library in his town contains. And to estimate ten books read with care in a year may be to place the figure too high. Then again, after thirty years of reading, this regular reader might find more pleasure in going back and rereading books he had enjoyed in his youth than in moving on to new ones.

Fortunately, books are like foreign countries or parts of your own land that you have never visited. You do not have to travel over them mile by mile to get a reasonably adequate idea of what they are like. The account of one honest traveler saves you that, especially if he knows you and has seen things through your eyes, as it were. Like many public figures, Edward VII never read anything because of lack of time, but he kept informed about everything that was published in his kingdom. While he smoked or was being shaved or having his beard trimmed, he peppered a reader with questions until he had his own clear notion of what a given book was about.

Essentially, this is a good method: to *ask* questions and to hear replies, for in this way you are never passive. A woman novelist confided to a friend: "Don't tell anyone, but I love the first and last twenty pages of a book best. The rest I make over for myself by daydreaming."

Marcel Proust's first book was a translation of Ruskin. Now, Proust did not know English very well, and someone has described him intently studying in Ruskin's text "those—for him—indecipherable pages which he nevertheless profoundly understood." Proust himself said, "There is no better way to become aware of one's own feelings than to try to re-create in oneself what a great master has felt. In making such a searching effort, we bring to light our own thought together with his. . . ."

There are obscure passages in any good book, which is good for the reader, for what you think you have understood at first glance will always remain opaque and unknown. The true reader's first impression upon reading a work of genius should be more or less, "Yes, it's beautiful, but it is difficult, too."

## II

Religious writers who have discussed how to read a book in order to draw from it nourishment for the soul advise you to stop reading as soon as you feel moved. And indeed the most beautiful image you can imagine of the act of reading is the woman Corot painted as she sits dreaming or meditating, holding a book in which one finger marks the page where she broke off. Basically, what an author wants is to be completed, as it were, in another spirit. He offers you margins and spaces between lines where you can write down your thoughts among his own. Nothing is more touching than to see a book lying open at a page someone is reading attentively and to wait for the sound of the leaf that will not be turned.

Of course, if you pitched your tent every time you came to a passage that pleased you or made you think, you would never read. There is a story told of an early Church Father who wished to study and meditate upon the Lord's Prayer, and who after several years had not got beyond the words "Our Father"—which do indeed say everything. All the same, in order to understand a book well you must read it through, even if quickly, and absorb its particular rhythm so that the portions you prefer will be in context and illumined by the whole.

Descartes said of most books that "once one has read a few lines and looked at the indexes, [they] are known in their entirety," the rest having been added to fill up space. Recalling this, the French philosopher and author, Louis Lavelle, said that all books are weighed down with connective material. In which, I may add, books resemble the creation in that what binds together takes up more room than that which nourishes or acts.

To have a book stimulate you as much as possible, it is also advisable that you lend it voice—your own or sometimes another person's. The ancients are said to have read aloud even when they were alone. Rapid, cursive reading with the eyes and without sounding the words is a modern invention; this habit of reading only with the eyes, so precious and well suited to prose, makes you unresponsive to poetry and even to *number,* which is that part of poetry that exists in prose.

## III

A good book benefits you by making you share in the experience of another person, which in this world is hardly ever possible, even in the case of people nearest to you. (How are you ever to find your way through the mists of habit or reserve!) Often the people around you lack the mastery of language that would enable them to condense their own experiences, and so to you it seems that they have nothing to teach you. A book places you in the middle of an unfamiliar mind and then surrenders its very essence to you. You need to have tried your own hand at writing to imagine what scraps and waste one finished page implies, how much material has been condensed, how many even good things have disappeared to give resonance to those that remain. And even when the book makes no allusion to the private life of its author, there is hardly a page that does not presuppose some secret.

A genuine book is written out of necessity, as true reading is reading done out of hunger and desire. And if it is advisable to refrain from reading if you do not feel impelled to read, so you should forego writing a book if you are not convinced that you have something to communicate that no one else can say for you. This does not mean that every page of such a book will be new or personal. A book is never uniformly interesting or appealing; like the daily life of which it is the precipitate, it includes its boring, dull, and dismal moments, which are the precondition for the reawakening of inspiration.

This may give someone the idea of taking his scissors and cutting out some "selections" or of making condensations, as Americans were the first to do with their digests. But it is easy to see that a digest drains all flavor from a book; the process is rather like converting your daily meals into food capsules. As for selections or excerpts, by removing the terrain, the atmosphere, and the setting, they transform a living flower into a dried flower, yet this is considered fit fare to offer children or the foreigner. You have to resign yourselves to a book's being weak in spots; it will drag now and then, or be repetitious; it will suffer from omissions and gaps and many other flaws. Often the best books, those that have been most imitated, have very great flaws—witness the Bible or Plato. Anyone who is familiar with the genesis of a book, who knows the digressions that occur between the uncertainty of a manuscript and the eternally fixed text that is printed, bound, and distributed to all comers, has compassion for books and forgives much.

True readers love to go back to the same book; they will buy it even at a sacrifice or have it mended and rebound in order to keep it, day and night, near wherever it is they dream. There is a great difference between the book that is loaned to you and the book that belongs to you. Reading implies your being able to know that such and such are the pages you particularly cherish and being able to find them without too much difficulty. At one extreme, you will read only one book in your whole life, like the ancient Jews, or certain Christians, or like the French writer, M. de Saci, who read St. Augustine exclusively, but derived from him enough wit and wisdom to stand up to Pascal. Some books that are rather

dull in themselves could be filled with light if you resolved to read them and them only through a lifetime
and to ask how, in their terms, you can interpret the
meaning of your life experiences. People are occasionally
amazed that Hegel or Marx have this potential, but
actually obscurity or voluminousness or gaps (witness
the brevity of aphorisms) in a book are characteristics
that help us to find lodging in it for our own thoughts.
The hermetic book is the one from which you take or to
which you give the most.

The books you should keep by your bedside are the
ones that can, no matter what the circumstances, give
you guidance or helpful stimulus: they may uplift you
by relating the life of some admirable man; they may
speak of a man much like yourselves and thereby reassure you—Montaigne is a case in point; they may reveal
to you the universe as it really is; they may let you
share in the lives of other people in other places or other
times; and there are those that summarize the All, those
that sing. Perhaps the most beautiful book is one that
is not written to be read but is published after its author's death and, unshadowed by any wish to please, has
the quality of a testament. It is good, too, when the
book is old enough to have no links with the details of
your present life, for then it can make you feel that
whatever disturbs you in a present moment is a passing
thing.

You open some bedside books almost daily. Others you
hardly ever open, yet they exist and are very real for
you, and you know you could consult them any time.
They are like the people you never see but who do you
good simply because they exist and you know that to
see them you have only to knock at their door. Sometimes an author's name or title that awakens associations is enough.

And since in this as in all things the reverse is almost

equally true, I would say, "Keep for your bedside reading the book of your most incisive and most reasonable opponent—the way Pascal had Montaigne, and Montaigne, Seneca." It's a good thing to keep near you that insolent creature who pricks you on your weak points and forces you to search for solid proofs, who sees black where you see white. In this way you can better enjoy what you truly possess or moderate your certainties.

## IV

People have always loved to read fiction. They expect to find in fiction a more personal and a more vast truth, one closer to their hearts than so-called historical truth.

Anyone with experience in telling or writing stories could explain this. He knows that it is harder to tell a story than to present facts or to develop pure ideas. Fiction demands the same abilities of observation and abstraction, but to a livelier degree. You cannot tell a story well without investing the emotions of your characters with a density they do not have in daily life, without modifying or enlarging or narrowing them—and this without manipulating chance more propitiously than in real life. When you do this, you are moving in the direction of truth. Essentially, the storyteller's art is like the art of God, insofar as God predestines; that is, He creates events to the measure of human beings, and does so while apparently indifferent to man and his world. The storyteller, too, must have this air of being absent, this candor, this phlegm with regard to what he relates, whether it be terrible or touching—in a word, a kind of nonchalance, which is an attribute of sovereignty. He and he alone knows how it will all end. And since our storyteller survives to tell his tale, the reader-listener guesses that things will work out not too badly.

A storyteller beguiles his listener by telling him of a life similar to but more highly colored than his own—for example, the story of Abraham or Ulysses. So it is quite inadequate to define a novel, as does the Webster Unabridged, as "a fictitious prose tale of considerable length, in which characters and actions professing to represent those of real life are portrayed in a plot." The artist's imagination does not invent reality; his is a more arduous kind of observation. After each of his many political crises, Disraeli used to write a novel intended less for other readers than for himself; he was trying to understand, via a work of fiction, what had just happened to him, and what it was that he had dreamed but not really known in that state of sonambulism which is intense action. Had Disraeli had the gifts of a Balzac, his books would have enriched mankind even more than his career as statesman did. Most great deeds have been performed so that their authors could tell about them one day—as Joinville put it, "in the apartments of the ladies."

You must read novels to learn the meaning of your own life and the lives of those around you, for the dullness of daily routine masks it. You must read novels in order to penetrate social circles different from your own and there discover, through contrasts in customs, the alikeness of human nature; to study, as if in a laboratory, the fundamental human problems, which are those of sin, love, and destiny—study them in concrete terms, that is, and without the transpositions worked by morality. And, finally, you read to enrich your life with the substance and magic of other lives.

It is not without reason that the greatest success comes to those who know how to tell a good story—witness men like Homer, Cervantes, or Victor Hugo. Talent in this field is, you must admit, very rare. Every generation produces clever men who can record on page two the solution to the problem they have stated on page one, but this is only the mechanical part of storytelling. The hard thing is to know how to slip into your plot (which is a kind of human bookkeeping) a truth, a real character, a mysterious seed.

Today writers inject philosophy and psychology into the novel, whereas formerly authors preferred morality or the casuistry of the heart. In doing this, they ignore the essential rule of the genre, which is to have no other avowed purpose than to tell a story and to give pleasure. Unquestionably, philosophy and morality radiate from a good tale, but the characters should no more think about such things—nor should the author—than actors should remain aware that people are watching them and that they are acting.

History must be a part of your reading, too. Here your interest is centered on things that have actually taken place. It would be ideal if what really happened and what is subsequently related about it should turn out to have, in addition, the appeal of a novel. This happens only in what we in France call *"la petite histoire"*—informal and anecdotal—in contradistinction to *"la grande histoire"*—a comprehensive, methodical, and factual account. In *la grande histoire* events must obey their own law and not the law of art. History is necessarily austere, you might even say tedious, in which respect it resembles descriptive science. History must include sequences of events, enumerations, dates and details that are put on the same plane as great turning points in world affairs; what is important is put on a par with what is not. You find this even in a great historian like Tacitus, for all that he was also such an artist. People who read history must have the same kind of patience as the historian who writes it.

Also, I should point out that good popular books on

history compress and condense events. They allow you to witness the full span of a human life in the precipitous space of a few hours, or force you to embrace several centuries in a glance. Scholars, of course, dare not make such syntheses. The popular historians then borrow from the scholars' long and patient labor and win prominence in their stead. The public, however, is not wrong to ask for short and compact historical books. It is the scholars who are wrong not to supply such in their free time. What the educated public asks of the historian is not exhaustive and infallible detail but truthfulness in the long view.

## V

It is also a good idea occasionally to read a sound but nontechnical scientific book, so long as you understand it in the main but do not worry about grasping every point, which spoils any reading. No fiction can broaden your view in the same way as some knowledge of mathematics, physics, or biology.

Remarkably enough, with the exception of books on geometry, scientific books do not last more than thirty years. Knowledge that seems to be the most unassailable is the knowledge that spoils most quickly. Nothing is more dated than a scholarly scientific work that appeared, say, in the early twentieth century; one small discovery can make it obsolete forever, whereas poetry and philosophy never age. This is because exact works—of science or criticism—employ many symbols, while books dealing with metaphysics or the study of man have immediately accessible substance. It is strange that to us the Greeks seem to have been born yesterday, and although they knew nothing of what we know today, they can still show us the inner springs of being or human nature or politics. Zola as compared to Homer, or Bergson compared to Plato, is ancient.

Scholarly books put you off partly because they employ abstract language. They do not speak of Jones but of mankind, or essence or matter or else relationship. It is as if philosophers substitute for real and savory objects opaque phantoms created in their own brains. And it is true, as I have said elsewhere, that it is far easier to write a dissertation than a story, for abstract style is an inner music that is readily engendered of itself. Certain languages—the Germanic, for example— have such an affinity for abstract expression that although the person speaking it enunciates and seems to be thinking, he is only constructing a sentence. In other languages, like Greek or French, abstract words are close enough to common usage to preserve the flavor of the concrete thing, yet at the same time are transparent enough to denote the interior of the thing and its hidden resemblance to other things. You find this is true if you read Descartes, Malebranche, Ravaisson, or Lavelle. Lavelle has gone so far as to say that abstract words act miraculously on our spirit solely by virtue of their presence.

Furthermore, no one should suppose that to understand a philosopher's thought thoroughly you must always look for a philosophic system or a nugget of pure truth. Alain was an accomplished reader who knew even better how to teach other people to read, and he recommended that one sometimes read Kant the way one reads Montaigne or Proust. Neither philosophers nor novelists, he observed, tell you what they really think, the first because they believe they should conceal it, and the latter because they get carried away by their story; in both cases, the reader must catch them out, waiting for a moment of forgetfulness when they will give themselves away. Even in books of pure thought, like the "Ethics"

or "Creative Evolution," the philosophic system con-
ceals some individual human experience that has been
developed to the highest degree of generality. Today it
has come to a point where a philosopher can choose
his vehicle indifferently among abstract treatise, novel,
film, or theater. Actually, it should be possible to trans-
pose any form of expression into another. It is challeng-
ing to search for the philosophy of a novel or for the personal history hiding within an abstraction.


# VI


You may well wonder what would have become of
the Christian faith if it had not had the scriptures to
sustain it. Religion teaches you to read; it teaches you
that what truth and beauty there may be in a given
work does not come from its author. A believer believes
that the Bible was written by the Infinite for him. He
has the idea (irrefutable, for that matter) that if the
Spirit once inspired Isaiah, that same Spirit has also
chosen this moment or this chapter and verse (which he
happens on by chance) to give *him* comfort and a kind
of second inspiration.

A religious or mystical book does not benefit only
the man who has faith. Every man is religious to the
extent that he is capable of attention and silence. The
resemblance between attention and prayer has often been
noted, although it is often forgotten by both parties—
that is, by the believer who indulges in prayer inatten-
tively and the nonbeliever who is satisfied with attention
unaccompanied by prayer.

The spirit of religion is not so remote from that of
science when science is seeking to move forward. "Eleva-
tion," Novalis said, "is the most excellent means I
know of to avoid fatal collisions. For example, the ele-

vation of all citizens to the rank of noblemen, of all men to genius, of all phenomena to the state of mystery."

In our civilization, the Bible is the book *par excellence*. And the remarkable thing is, it is not a book at all but a collection of all forms of writing except the abstract. In one small volume, it contains every form of speech from code of law to love song, passing en route through calm proverbs, lamentations, parables, and bloody and brutal narratives.

The art of reading, then, if I have made myself clear, consists in composing a second bible for yourselves. The first you read with intelligence; the second—your own— you read with faith.

# 7

# Seeds and Husks

Once when I was making a retreat, I found on the table in my cell an unused notebook with these words from the Bible printed on the cover: "Gather up the broken pieces that are left over, so that nothing may be wasted." (John, 6:12). This is Jesus speaking, after He has multiplied the loaves and fishes. Why, following a feat in which He produced so abundantly, should He counsel picking up the leavings? It is up to the exegetes —perhaps even more to the mystics—to explain that for us, but it is quite clear that here is richly helpful advice to guide the work of the mind. Illumination is a passing thing at best, and you must always be picking up the pieces afterward. This is a commonplace experience you are all familiar with from your earliest school days, for even as children you have to provide for the future—that is, think ahead, formulate and state precisely what is happening now to prevent its being hopelessly forgotten.

What symbols or tokens can you use to gather together the work of the mind? How can you pin down ideas of your own or of someone else so that you can re-examine and ponder over them—go back, that is, to something you once knew and cherished, for this is the essence of knowing?

Lamartine said, "Make a mirror for your life."[1] He himself kept a daily record of what he had done with a given day.

Keeping a diary that no one will ever see is a useful habit—to write for yourself, that is, and for the angels. On the other hand, some famous contemporaries—Gide, Maurois, Marcel Green, for example—publish their journals. This wins them many unknown, silent friends, for everyone loves to know what comes to an author on the spur of the moment that he records without fore-thought or correction. But everyone can benefit from keeping a journal if he wants to. Young people should be urged to prepare this secret soil which they can come back to later, to learn to know themselves and also to find working materials that bear their own imprint and have already acquired a patina of age.

Modesty can sometimes get in the way; you may feel that writing down your thoughts is like dressing them up for others to see. Some people would rather bury them forever; others jot them down, crumple the paper, and throw it away. Still others carefully record what they believe is most intimately and peculiarly their own only to discover some years later how banal their thoughts were. If only sincerity were needed to be original, we would all be artists!

If your sense of modesty makes you hesitate to record personal things, you can begin by copying passages from authors you have liked—a few sentences, a line or two from a poem, perhaps just a phrase you have found useful—and venture now and then to speak for yourself

[1] "Do as I do—make a mirror for your life. Give one hour to writing down your impressions and to a silent examination of conscience. . . . It is pleasant to preserve the happy moments that slip from us or the tears we have shed, in order to find them again, a few years later, and to say to ourselves, So that's what made me so happy that day! That is what I cried over! This teaches us how unstable are both feelings and things."

in the margin. You can mention daily events—where
you have been, whom you have seen. It is very pleasant,
later, to have these landmarks. Your forebears used to
keep such personal or family records. Each life had
its own logbook.

After what Vergil calls "the long forgettings," these
diaries or journals or calendars allow you to discover
the pleasures of remembering. Such a retracing keeps
things from evaporating, as memories have a way of
doing. It also keeps the thing remembered within the
range of present attention, colors it with your whole
spirit. A simple recollection is transformed into nourishment for the inner life.

The Jews have spent twenty centuries remembering!
Even their prayers are generally a reliving of their
wonderful and tragic history. Jacob *thought* God when
he recalled God's behavior in the Abraham and Isaac
story; God made Himself manifest in the experiences
of the patriarchs, especially when they were called and
when they died. Christ is to all appearances absent from
the present day, yet He is eternally active; as Newman
said, He is manifest in memory. This may be taken
symbolically; people who are afraid of the word "Christ"
can substitute "sense of destiny" or "self-knowledge,"
which is hidden from you at the moment a given experience occurs but is released to you through intelligent
remembering.

If a man rereads a ten-year-old diary, he rediscovers
a tranquil, complete, and resolved part of his own life,
which, like everything that is forever closed, has rich-
ness, order, and beauty. (This is even truer of a diary
that antedates the great changes we have known—a
diary written, say, before 1914, in the era of gracious
living, or before 1939, when the word "freedom" still
had real meaning.) This man can even detect prefigura-
tions of what was to happen to him—initial situations,

themes of joy and surprise and grief that have appeared more than once in the interim and will no doubt appear again in the course of his life. He may glimpse, too, a prefiguring of the final moments of his life.

It is impossible to cite personal examples other than those literature has given. A long time ago, when I was reading St. Augustine's "Confessions," I was struck by their prophetic nature, since even before his conversion they anticipated things to come. Had Augustine kept a diary (and he may well have), at forty-five he could have read early entries that outlined what was to happen to him at the pivotal point in his life. Judging from his behavior as a young bishop, he was moved then by the same impulses, temptations, thoughts, and fantasies that had characterized his adolescence. (This suggests that sin is not only original but constant.) By looking for signs and footprints in the almost automatic account of your own past actions, good, bad, or indifferent, you become aware of your own identity. And why do you enjoy reading novels if not for the pleasure of witnessing an imaginary life unfold, of being able to observe the early forecasts and the ultimate accomplishments and measuring how they balance out. Since no one is his own best friend, however, you do not do for the one being who is real to you what you are pleased to admire in imaginary characters.

Furthermore, when you re-examine the traces of your own past, you discover that its meaning changes. This helps you to understand how Proust's Normandy childhood and the death of his grandmother did not mean the same thing to him every time he resuscitated those early experiences. Or how, if he had reread the death of Bergotte or of his grandmother as he himself lay dying, he would have found in them presages of his own death. In the same way, the 1914 diary reread in 1939 has one meaning, reread in 1945 has another, and

reread in 1969 will have still another. All of which suggests that if the past cannot be changed, it is a moist
clay that can assume different shapes according to your
state of mind at a given moment.

"Keep daily notes," Max Jacobs said, "neat, legible
notes with exact dates. If I had kept a diary day by day,
today I would have a whole encyclopedia. One word
re-creates a whole atmosphere. Oh, how much we lose!
*What* jewels are lost! . . . Be sure to keep a journal of
your life. Like this:

"June 22: Today studied bones of the leg. . . . Super-
intendent said to me, 'You put money in the bank a
penny at a time, like an eye dropper.' . . . Professor *X*
has a nose as big as Pinocchio's. He's forever striking
poses, wants to impress the students. . . . Read *X* book
on *X*. . . . Remembered such and such. . . . Had lunch
with *A* (give a sketch of *A*). . . . Stopped by the court-
house and listened for a while to the trial of (give details of trial). . . ."

If, like Alphonse Daudet, you make sure that nothing
you have seen is allowed to be lost, you will obviously
have material for several novels. This is the secret of
many authors. They let nothing slip away; for them
there is no such thing as a crumb; no scrap of reality
is too trivial. For the philosopher, too, there are no
notions that may not develop into an idea.

Now that all this has been said, I must point out
that there is an entirely different breed of mind which
finds that the act of writing works mischief and actually
disperses thought.

One such person wrote me this: "If I write things
down, it makes me feel as if I have discharged my ideas,
driven them from my mind and loosed them to the
four winds. Writing deprives them of all life and motion. That's why at a lecture I never take notes. I listen,
let myself be carried along. Sometimes I admire what

I hear, sometimes I understand it (aha!) in a flash, but it stays with me forever. Bothering with paper and pen would keep me from thinking. When I do write, it's in a very small notebook, and just a date or a formula or a cryptic reference as a reminder. I have no more exams to pass, of course, and no one is going to cross-question me any more—and I don't have the thankless job of being a writer!

"All I want and need to do is to be able to think, and I notice that no matter what the subject is, I learn more from the way in which something is said than from the substance of it. The gist of the topic scarcely matters; what makes me think is the way the subject is developed and put to me, the form in which it is clothed. The modern method is not for me. Or rather, I would say that the moderns—the existentialists, for example—do not have exactly that which is ordinarily called style: they want to hit us with the very things themselves. But I belong to the old school which believes that on the whole things are unimportant and is interested only in what is incidental to the subject. This being the case, why should I take notes or keep notebooks? I will do thinking enough without."

This method, which asks only that the pen record essentials in the form of excerpts or maxims, is not to be scorned. It was the method of the Elders and Kings, of Solomon and David. In our garrulous day, when virtually every candidate for a degree wants to see himself in print, it is no longer fashionable. A book today is an excrescence; to produce one, you must learn to fill up so and so many pages. Once upon a time, on the contrary, you had to learn to restrain yourself, to suggest the maximum with little.

I watched another friend of mine over a period of years as he rigorously studied and prepared himself for high administrative office. This man wrote only when it was absolutely indispensable. Whatever his current post was, he always organized around him a small core of solid, sympathetic minds; he assigned specific research projects, and his criticism of the reports and recommendations that resulted was stringent, but then he would delegate authority to act while he himself withdrew and disappeared, rather like a god retiring behind the storm clouds. He never read a newspaper; he had the papers read and digested for him. He never called conferences to address them but rather for his own benefit; he found it useful to have information filtered through another mind, like the cabinet minister listening to his bureau chief. I used to notice how, when he was reading or thinking, he would jot down a few words on little scraps of paper. Then he would throw the scraps away. When I asked why this labor of Penelope, he said that one is too much the prisoner of a written text. To his way of thinking, it was better to form solid, substantial ideas that could be modified in response to a given situation and not to be the uneasy slave of one's own notes. You do better by yourself and by others, he used to say, when you're fighting with your back to the wall.

This brought to mind a comparable experience I'd had when teaching in a secondary school. Once, toward the end of the term, I had occasion to ask the students which of our sessions together they remembered best. They confessed that in their nascent, albeit great, forgetfulness they really remembered only one lesson; it had been in February, and they could even pinpoint the date. I was so touched that I flushed. Out of the entire year, that was the day that had found me least prepared and I had met with them feeling harassed and empty; but since I had, after all, to conduct a class, I had risen to the occasion by dredging ideas from my very entrails.

I have observed at first hand an English statesman

who followed similar methods: no current reading of his own but much conversation about other people's reading, he being always careful to make them talk without his risking the contributions that give one away. If common civility or official responsibility forced him to express an opinion, he did so, and while the form was always clear the content was rather reserved and obscure so as not to arouse strong feelings and to maintain flexibility in relation to the double face of the future. Once, when he was with the Foreign Office and in the midst of a very critical situation, I remember seeing him walk by some newspapers that were lying on a table. "I never read a paper," he said. "How can one write the truth when one must write every day and without the perspective of time?"

The ancients hardly ever wrote. The Elders of Israel never wrote at all. Jesus never wrote except once, and that was on sand, while He was talking with the adulteress. Socrates did not write, either. And the farmer, the sailor, the soldier, the meditative man—none of them writes. God inspires, but He does not write.


### III


Now that you have considered methods that are contrary to the ones I recommend, I feel free to speak of current common practices that consist in keeping a lasting record of your ideas.

I see two distinct reasons for collecting and keeping them.

First, they encourage concentration by providing an accompaniment that keeps your attention from wandering. Many people find that they must write in order to think. The very act of putting the thing down in words forces them to externalize what would otherwise

remain inside forever. Writing allows you to summarize
your ideas and find your own direction. If speech sustains you, what you write does so even more. Also, it
gives you the assurance that your ideas will endure for
you and for others. It consoles you for that sense of
evanescence which is implicit in the fugitive act of
thinking.

The act of writing encourages moderation, too, for,
leaping over the intervals, thoughts move all too quickly
from one extreme to another. But when you write, you
have to use the old, old words with their multiple nuances and the often burdensome, bizarre spelling that
is their peculiar luxury. Respect for the meaning and
the spelling of words leads you from solitary exercise
back into the areas of common usage and in so doing
operates as a helpful check and control.

Lastly, writing is a relief; it lifts the inexpressible or
indescribable weight that has been oppressing you. It
feels good to pick up a pen and tell, teach, remember,
forecast—with complete freedom. The first thing a dictator does is confiscate pens, as we in France learned
in 1940.

One thing is certain: notes must be held to a minimum. I am not talking now about the notes you take
in the course of a scholarly project. If you are putting
together a dictionary, you must have as many entry
cards for each word as that word has meanings and
uses. But as a student you have little or nothing to do
with such patient scholarship, which, for that matter,
is usually undertaken in teams, with a whole army of
faithful beaters and bearers. What you do ask of your
intelligence is that, with the help of other minds, it produce a work on which it will have left its mark. That
is why I say notes should be few in number; they form
an image of what you remember which, if you wish to
remain sane, must be selective and succinct.

You must be cautious about acquiring information that is not connected with earlier knowledge, that cannot be adapted or assimilated to what you already possess. Information that cannot be added to and incorporated with other data seems to me more harmful than useful. Information that you cannot relate to the categories of knowledge you cherish, that has not got some proportion, relevance, and resemblance to yourselves, is of no use either. I am talking now of the information you accumulate in maturity, after the examinations and competitions are behind you; in your early years you must indeed amass information, but even then it is important to select insofar as possible what attracts, suits, and pleases, you.

If you apply these rules to notes, you will conclude that a useful note is one that deals with the type of information you will most need and that is at the same time an image of your own mentality. The acme of perfection is the note that has the greatest potential usefulness—one, I mean, that has multiple value and can be utilized in various projects. Your file of notes should be like reserve troops—that is, a stock you always have at hand and keep in constant readiness, so that they can be thrown into action when and if the tide of battle turns against you. And the best reserve troops are those that can intervene here, there, and everywhere, under the most varied circumstances.

I used to like to make very brief indications on my own cards, which I called "compasses" because they pointed out the various ways in which the information on that particular card could be used. Here is one example, which I used in my class in ethics. I had taken the note while reading a book on the evolution of law. It dealt with mediaeval practices in lending money at interest. Such a loan, says my note, was condemned by theologians in line with the principle of justice which

says that to demand interest on money one has loaned
is to abuse the poor—which was undeniable, at the
time, since silver and gold did not then have value
in themselves. The law authorized interest to be charged,
my note reads on, in only three cases: in the event of
a loss of profit (*lucrum cessans*); in the event of dam-
ages that could be shown to have actually arisen (*dam-
num emergens*); and in the event the loaner risked not
recovering the money from his debtor (*periculum sortis*).
Economic conditions have since changed, and the exception has become the rule; what was once unjust has
come to be considered just—not because principles of
justice have changed but because currency has acquired
value. This is the summary of ideas and facts contained
in one note. My "compass"—in the upper-righthand corner—carries the following:

> Development
> Custom
> Application
> Rule
> Exception
> Ethics and sociology
> Idea of justice

For me these were indications of how the information
in that note could be variously used on those unknown
battlefields which are future classes, papers, and examinations.

Experience shows how hard it is to find fact-idea
combinations rich enough to be able to help you in
several ways. In whatever the subject, even in grammar, I have noticed that people find it very troublesome
to give a good example and generally try to avoid having to. Hence, a supply of meaningful, stimulating *versa-
tile* notes. Notes written on substantial paper, and to
the wide measure, since in that way they can be more
easily consulted. Notes that present *one idea only*, sup-

ported by one or more facts, or that present only one fact which contains one or more meanings. Notes that have succinct headings. Notes that are dated, so that you know at what stage in your life you made them. With exact references to the source from which you have taken them. All proper names printed, preferably. Notes that are legible, correctly punctuated, as transmissible as a bequest to a future heir—notes that are both provisional and everlasting.

## IV

An old college friend whom I ran into recently said, "I've kept one good habit from those days. Even now, when I want to learn something I go back to it. It's the outline, roman numeral one, sub-point A.

"It's a calligraphic picture, with words written in red or underlined, which you can look at again and again. (However, you must have prepared it yourself. I've noticed that an outline made by someone else is nowhere nearly so useful.) This kind of picture makes you learn and understand simultaneously. It serves the same purpose as the graph in statistics or geometry. It lets you see things at a single glance. This is a big advantage it has over the manual, which discusses things one by one, page by page, and doesn't enable you to judge proportion and relation.

"When my outlines are finished," my friend went on, "I pin them up on the wall, and learn by glancing at them now and then. For example, I took a professor's advice and made an outline of German grammar on a single page. If one page is enough for German grammar, you can imagine what this method can do! Naturally, when you make an outline you must simplify, but to simplify is to look for the essence of the thing.

The art of simplifying together with the art of developing, which is just the reverse, make up the art of learning, which we have to practice all our life. If you want to learn something at your age—there's a lot of satisfaction in learning at the age of fifty—sit down and make an outline.

"Say, for example, that you want to learn the history of such and such a country. You begin by setting up for yourself (No crutches! Walk on your own two feet) a synoptic chronology. You will divide your paper into several columns: one is for military events; one is for diplomacy; one is for foreign relations; one is for religious developments; the fifth is for creative activity in the arts; the sixth for scientific advances, and so on. You will discover that even if you are mature and already have some knowledge of the field, a chronology of this kind can teach you new things. The lines of influence have been traced and you have only to underline them. The role that chance plays often comes out more clearly. And all the inter-relationships, too—how a small scientific invention will pass almost unnoticed but, after a lapse of time, will be translated into a weapon and used in a battle that topples empires.

"I use the same method in geography. If I want to study the province of Brittany, instead of making a single map of Brittany and putting everything on it, as I used to do, now I make ten or so rough maps—absolute exactness doesn't matter, for each outline should be stylized. On one I put, for example, rivers and coastline; on another, cities and highways; on another, forests and so forth; on another, the route that Patton's Fifth Army followed. What is the advantage of this system? Each map represents a single concept. Each one has to do with a fact illuminated by an idea, for I make each one correspond to an easily found principle. But—and I must repeat this—like a graph, an outline is use-

less if it is the work of someone else. There would be
no point in my buying readymade maps or tables. Everyone must be his own teacher and pupil."

# 8

# Notes and

# Courses

Stendhal used to begin a new piece of writing with a summary. Then he interleaved the summary with blank pages on which he wrote his comments and observations. This procedure, he realized, had the disadvantage of making his borrowings too apparent. Whether one is writing history, poetry, or fiction, one does need sources, but we find it important to dissimulate this fact. For his purposes, Stendhal invented the file card. According to Jean Prévost, from whom I have borrowed these details, the file card provides modern historians with "the means of pulverizing the source books they use into fragments—into a sentence, a date, a single fact—and of readily combining several sources to get not a patchwork but well-mixed colors; in this way, they need less wit to appear more original." This would sound quite unscrupulous only if you were to surrender to the common hypocrisy which pretends that a work of the intelligence does not borrow from others. We know quite well, however, that a work of art is often an adept transposition of old materials enriched by several distinguishing differences on which an individual genius has put its mark.

A file card, in my terms, is nothing more than a note arranged vertically. The vertical classification has advantages. It allows you to order and control your material better, to rearrange it easily, make it more flexible, more mobile—like the mind itself.

For the note to become a file card, however, several precautions must be taken.

The format of your cards must be the same from your youth until the end of your days. What size does not much matter; the important thing is that it be always the same. Whether you arrange your cards in cardboard, wood, or metal files, nothing is more impractical than a card that does not fit your standard format. It is about as useless as a shell that does not fit the caliber of the cannon. *Quidquid non juvat obstat.* So choose your format as early as possible and then stick with it.

I should mention a second rule, I think, although it is less indispensable. The ideal card is one you slip into your pocket, or one that you can fit into the inside pocket of a loose-leaf notebook.

It is hard to believe how much information you can get onto one small card. If you need more space, you take a second, mark it "2," and so on. You could write the whole "Discourse on Method" on cards arranged in sequence.

A well-taken note should be potentially useful to your friends and descendants. In fact, if several of you were to choose the same size for your files, and make yourselves write legibly (as if you were taking your manuscript to your publisher forthwith), it would be possible to work together. I don't put much faith in projects that involve thinking together. When you want to learn, you must become disciples. Thought is dissipated in talk, and for conversation to be profitable you must talk with a sincere and perspicacious opponent. Even in this case, I think it is better to write than to talk things out. Perhaps with a close friend, but there again it would be better to be together in silence. You can lend one another books, however, audit each other's courses, and exchange class notes as well as other information.

It is a good idea to carry with you always a package of file cards of the size you have chosen to be yours for life. The advantage here is that you can catch the phrase or fact or fresh idea on the wing. An idea comes to you the way the Day of the Last Judgment will come—unexpectedly. A formula, a line, a date, a detail, a clarification, a figure—sometimes that's all you need to summarize a piece of work or to make a start. A man's fate occasionally depends on his having his name in his pocket and its being put into the hands of the man or woman looking for him. Thought is fugitive; the mind does not repeat itself; if you do not catch the whisperings of the oracle as they come to you, they are lost forever. You must—and this is absolutely essential—convince yourselves that what is offered you this very moment will never be offered again. That which is missed now is forever missed. But thanks to the little packet of cards of the proper size, a line that is written now is written forever. There will be no need to recopy, which is one of the most distasteful jobs in the world. And when you reach home, you can decide on the right place for this note in your file—which I myself often think of as a honeycomb into which I can dip as needed. The moment of taking the note will very likely correspond to the moment (perhaps several years later) when you will put it to use. These little tricks of management are calculated to save time ·and also to give to the passing moment a small measure of perenniality.

Cards of small—and standard—format allow you to

take notes everywhere: on a bustling street, in an airplane, during a wakeful moment in the night, and especially, of course, during your classes and study periods.


## II


Now I would like to quote some advice given me almost forty years ago by Professor Félix Boillot, of the University of Bristol, who spent his life studying methods of intellectual work.

"The way to create a good method for yourself is very simple," he told me. "It is to analyze systematically the way you have worked up to that point. You must examine, one by one and in the most minute detail, all the phases of your intellectual activity, and do this with inexorable severity, as if you were paying a lot—and you are paying a lot!—to discover your weak points and how to correct them. You must be able to put your pride in your pocket really to do this—and what is rare, you must really want to know." For his own benefit, Félix Boillot made an intensive investigation of how great industrial enterprises in both France and the United States are run, as well as the diplomatic services and the general staffs of several nations, and on the basis of this study he evolved a personal work method that eliminated waste of time and effort. He had given particular thought to Gutenberg's invention of the movable-type press. This is the story, as he used to tell it:

Johann Gutenberg, who was born apparently as ingenious as he was industrious, wracked his brain for years to find some way of copying material without having to use a pen, since that meant being able to make only one copy at a time. About a hundred years earlier, the Dutch had invented the wood-block process; with an awl they hollowed a block of wood so as to raise the outline of the design or word that was to be reproduced. The raised surfaces were then inked and the face of the block was pressed against a sheet of white paper. Gutenberg kept turning this process over and over in his mind. Very difficult to apply to book production, for there would be so many blocks to cut. Even for a very little book, what an expense! And the blocks could never be reused to produce other books. "But," thought Gutenberg, "suppose one were to break the blocks down. What if, instead of cutting words on blocks, I were to cut each letter on a small separate block. Then if I arranged and aligned these, each block carrying just one of the twenty-four letters of the alphabet, I would be able to compose any page whatever. I could make as many copies as I wanted—a thousand or ten thousand—and then demobilize my letters and remobilize them to make different words and different lines for a new book. Basically, nothing could prevent my reproducing all the manuscripts in the world in as many copies as I'd like and at very little cost."

Félix Boillot conceived an analogous idea. He said to himself: "What are books or the chapters of books made of? For that matter, what are our ideas made of? Of more elementary thoughts, of facts, or of experiences—of widely assorted data. These elements are bound together, and it is as impossible to break them apart as, before Gutenberg, it was impossible to separate the elements of the wood block. But let's suppose that I break my ideas down into elements, and suppose I assign each element a piece of paper the size of a playing card. Then I would be able, once I'd finished a given piece of writing, to demobilize the elements that had served for this particular piece of work, send them back to their hearths like so many released soldiers—in other words, classify them in some order, alphabetical or chronological, say, and remobilize them when and as I find I need them. I can do the same while reading. I will not put all my notes in one book or memorandum; I will de-compose them and, like Descartes, multiply them 'into as many parcels as possible' and to each *un*decomposable fact I will assign a card. At the top of this card I will put an easily-read heading that indicates the content; one word will often be enough. And after reading for an hour, instead of having filled two pages with notes I will have filled perhaps a dozen cards."

## III

The arrangement of notes or cards follows a very simple principle: a note is well classified when it is quickly findable.

The best method of classification would be the one that allowed you to locate in the space of ten seconds, after an interval of ten years, any note whatever. This much having been said, it is quite possible that for some mentalities the best method of arranging notes may be not to take any but to settle for a kind of logbook. One should attempt the card-filing system only if one has an orderly, methodical mind, for filing, like any action that is essentially elegant and luxurious, does not admit of mediocrity. It is better to classify nothing than to classify badly. And there is, after all, the natural and essential classification of time and chronology. If you were not born methodical, I would say to you, "Don't force yourself. Write things down as they happen, day by day. You will remember that such and such a note was jotted down the day you visited the Bastille in 1789 or during the Revolution, in

1848, and turn accordingly to your logbook for '89 or your file drawer for '48."

And to confound our methodical friends, I want parenthetically to tell a true story. I was full of admiration for the books of Père Emile Lagrange, so when I was in Jerusalem I went to see him. Many of his books presuppose considerable documentation, as evidenced in footnotes and even notes to footnotes. (I have in mind his commentaries, like shafts of rose granite, on the four Gospels.) I was curious to see this scholar at work. I visualized series of boxes on his desk, all of them neatly filled with cards. Reality was quite different. The Father had a large notebook in which he had written the excerpts from texts that he intended to quote; he had written them as he read, and in no particular order, but he had indicated every source. I didn't see a single loose card or note; everything was in that one big ledger. This was the method of Tillemont and, very likely, all the old historians. A good memory is worth more than any classification system.

For people who do not trust their memories, the well-indexed card is a necessity. Often it is not possible to work out a rational, specialized classification in advance, so the best provisional order is alphabetical or chronological. The big advantage to cards is that you can change the order of classification when you want to; indeed, cards rather ask to be mixed together and re-assorted. This is a good thing to do when you are feeling a little tired.

The 100 per cent methodical minds will want to adopt the decimal system, which can be applied to every kind of classification. You will find the principles of this method in books more learned than this one.

Once your cards are arranged, you may find it pleasantly useful to subdivide them by small tabs that are available in plastic or cardboard. Blue tabs, say, for the

ones you think most important, or, if you have set
your cards up in an historical, chronological sequence,
for those that relate to the same idea. These tabs establish different axes for a given group of cards, making them in this resemble the world of nature where
things are not linear but multiple. Every thing, every living being, every circumstance belongs to not one but
several series. It is you who artificially impose a single
seriation; chiefly, it is the artifice of words that, acting
like a resonant chain of single meanings, forces your
thoughts to unfold in a single linear direction. Movable
cards actually invite you to upset this particular order
and recompose it differently. The tabs, without disturbing a provisional order, allow you to plot other
series, other possible mobilizations.

The card file is certainly not the only imaginable
system. People of artistic temperament or some who
are put off by the idea of a strict order often prefer
notebooks. These have the great advantage of being
big enough to accommodate long notes and even clip-
pings. Admittedly, the short note eliminates context
and context is often indispensable.

In any event, your using this method or that is not
enough in itself to make you think. Yet thought is such
a subtle, infrequent breath that you never have ready
at hand enough ways to prepare for it, arouse it, show
it at its best, multiply it in all its manifold effects, and
pass it on to the largest possible number of other people. The virtue of economy counsels you to be always
on the lookout for ways to facilitate and maximize the
impact of your thoughts.

IV

And now we must discuss courses and lectures, thinking about them in relation to the listener and his mem-

ory. What conditions favor your chances of keeping a solid, lasting impression of what you hear—of being truly taught something? The pleasure of listening and the vague euphoria that come from a well-delivered lecture are not enough in themselves to teach you.

When I was teaching, I was devoted to an exercise that most people shrug off as stupid—dictation. In many cases, dictation is, I admit, the most hateful exercise there is. And yet classes cannot live in a state of perpetual effervescence. To Socratize tires both Socrates and Menon. The freshness of a new class is an admirable thing, but I wonder how long either teacher or students can keep up the pace. We must look ahead to the fact that after the gallop comes the trot, and after the trot a mere walk, not to mention the bag of oats. Five minutes of dictation offers this advantage. In dictation you find a rhythm that bears you up and along, a kind of gentle but productive drowsiness, quite like the effect produced by any sustained monotonous thing. Your spoken prayers, repeated again and again and again, are a dictation you make God submit to so that He will restore your peace.

I took care to dictate only noteworthy selections or ideas that sprang from me as fully formed and armed as Athena from the head of Zeus, so the students always knew that whatever they were writing down they should be sure to remember. I was also careful not to dictate very long at a stretch, and to interrupt the exercise by side remarks that were sometimes profound, or so I hoped, but again light and amusing or timely. (This was Montaigne's own method, although for himself he did just the opposite, and his way of resting was to recopy quotations from Latin writers he liked.) My rule was never to dictate a long passage and always to stop at the first sign of restlessness. Having taken these precautions, I found it a joy.

When the text was a quotation from some great thinker, there was no better way to give it its full flavor, I found, than to caress it with the voice, to make it unroll and flow in all its sonorousness. Dictation calls for an almost liturgical style of delivery, with the voice rising and falling and repeating the same thing in slight variation. This repetition is one way of driving the thing home to oneself, of presenting it in different aspects to one's own understanding. And all of this is done to the accompaniment of busily scratching pens as you look down over rows of bent and attentive young heads. And there are always the quick students who have finished a little sooner than the others and who sit waiting, their pens poised in air; and then there are the unruffled fellows who generally lag a little behind, having been too busy leaning over to copy their neighbor's paper. I made a point of giving punctuation: "comma . . . semicolon . . . dash." This lets the students catch their breath, but more importantly, in this way they also learn the art of punctuation, which, to my mind, is far more valuable than spelling. Spelling, after all, is a matter of remembering, but a feeling for the difference between "semicolon" and "colon" is a sign that you are thinking. And it is more valuable to think than to remember.

Insofar as possible, dictation exercises were kept in a separate notebook, one with heavier than ordinary paper, a more attractive—and hopefully a cleaner—cover. This notebook became a symbol of something that was to be preserved through all vicissitudes and handed down as a legacy to other sons of man.

I realize how far I am straying here from current methods in which there is greater concern to invent than to preserve, and I know that I must simply hold my peace until the great wheel of experience will have

made a half turn and the teacher come back to the
old way.

## V

Dare I go on now to say this? That I have never
liked the lecture course in which the teacher speaks
while the students "take notes"?

I am confident that short of having a professor who
speaks very slowly (as was the case with Bergson) it is
quite impossible to take notes as you listen. The pen
cannot write at the speed of speech. What happens is
that you barely pay any attention to the professor, because you are so intent on getting down in a barely
legible scrawl every word that falls from his lips. You
reread your notes later that evening, or never, or just
before an examination. You were not trying, however,
to grasp what he was saying but to snatch manna that
is not to be found in the textbook but may form the
basis of a final examination. If you are generous, you
will lend these scribblings to the poor devil who was
absent; this may spark gratitude, friendship, even a
marriage, but it is no road to knowledge. I know that
if Pascal had lectured, his slightest word, even if only
half remembered, would have had oracular weight.
But Pascal did not teach in high schools or colleges.

Note-taking, as it is practiced in most schools and
as it is, I believe, recommended by school authorities,
seems to me to be against nature. Unless the student
knows shorthand, he cannot keep up with the speaker
and, being always a bit behind, he is writing the sentence just finished while listening to the phrase that is
being pronounced. This division of attention cannot
be beneficial. True, practice makes perfect. Also, one
does find a few loquacious professors, born public speak-

ers rather than poets, who say the same thing three or four times. By writing only one of their two or three repetitive remarks, it is possible to get a fairly adequate train of thought down on paper. The ideal would be to imitate the mathematician, Henri Poincaré; he used to follow his courses at the Polytechnique with his eyes half closed and his arms crossed, and write out his notes immediately after the lecture. In this way, he got, as he used to say, "the order, which is even more important than the individual elements." When you are listening to a lecture, you must look for something quite different from what is readily to be found in your textbook. The lecturer is not a tutor, nor is he a talking book or a tape recording. If he is, then the one thing to do is to hear him out patiently and buy him, printed and bound, in the nearest bookshop.

If a professor's lecture amounts to more than his reading aloud, it is because as he speaks he is giving birth to something in himself; hence, the occasional fumbling, sudden flashes of feeling, pauses, unforeseen insights, hesitations. Young preachers and young teachers new to the exercise of speaking in public are afraid of stammering, of having to search for a word, of losing their train of thought for a moment. To avoid this awful risk, they learn their sermons by heart or they write out their lectures. They do not realize that in doing this they do indeed insure themselves against untoward accidents but also sacrifice the particular charm and usefulness of speech. When has a memorized or broadcast sermon ever converted anyone?

I don't believe that the public comes to a lecture to see the animal trainer devoured by the tigers of nerves and stage fright. But your pleasure at the circus would never be complete if at the back of your minds there was not always the thought that the acrobat might, just might make a false step on his tightrope—and that the professor at the university could find himself completely at a loss for words. This explains the special appeal of the speaker who arrives without notes, hangs up his hat and coat, and walking easily over to the lectern, snaps off the little reading lamp and begins to talk. You say to yourself, "He's made an awfully good beginning. Can he keep it up?" And he does, his sentences rising and receding like the tides.

I have noticed that a slight speech defect can actually be helpful in catching the listener's attention. Once he's become accustomed to it, he waits for it as if it gave a special flavor or were a kind of personal seal that any author puts on his work. Valéry had a slight stammer; Bergson had a special way of sucking in his breath; and these idiosyncracies were an essential part of their eloquence. To succeed means, in part, to accustom people to your faults and to make your public hanker after them like strong drink. Beginners are very wrong to worry so about speaking poorly; the only thing asked of them is that when they stand before you they be themselves. What the public does not forgive is a lack of naturalness; it overlooks personal faults provided one does not try to hide them. After all, people are all human.

This is said parenthetically to urge teachers to get as far away from their notes as they can, and "to give themselves to whatever comes," in Louis Lavelle's fine words. And I do not say that you should take no notes. You should note down everything that has to do with fact, date, quotation, or formula, especially if these are not to be found elsewhere. As for the teacher, when he is spelling something out precisely, he, like the traffic that slows down to pass a school building, should speak less quickly and even approximate the rather majestic delivery of the man who is dictating.

There are some subjects—the sciences and history, for

example—in which lectures are, as it were, the spoken first edition of a book that is still to be published. In such a case, you take down everything. I've gone so far as to say that a distinguished professor at the Ecole Normale prepared his courses so admirably and was such a miserable speaker that his students exempted him from lecturing and borrowed his wonderful notebooks instead. This was to the best interests of everyone concerned; the professor did not have to wear himself out and his students were sure of having a perfect and unpublished text, which they could draw on later for ideas with which to seed their own teaching. This is really an extreme case in which the very perfection of the preparation destroys the principle of the good lecture. What you seek in a course is communication of thought—the spirit of the word, not the letter, which in itself is generally sterile. And as can be verified time and again via radio broadcasts and telecasts, what you want more than to grasp a man's words is to sense his whole personality, which involves seeing him with our own eyes—his gestures, style, mannerisms, and weaknesses. To take notes now and then that will serve as vantage points; to let yourselves be permeated with ideas as they are presented; then, back in your own rooms, to reconstruct the lecture and record it clearly and concisely—this would indeed be the ideal way to follow courses that involve elements of taste and judgment rather than scholarship.

Obviously, to follow this method would make it impossible to attend many courses in a day; you might go to only two or three a week. What a blessing! Just as you drew a distinction between chore and work, so you could distinguish between lessons given by pedants and courses delivered by masters. In the first instance, you would take notes in some kind of personal shorthand and reserve the second method for the rare and magisterial experience.

## VI

Somewhere Montaigne wisely remarks that "even ashes have their value." One should never throw away so-called wastepaper; gather it up instead. You see the seed nourished on decomposed matter; tillable land is made from substances that have rotted. The tree finds its humus in its own dead leaves.

I think that everyone should keep, in his bottom drawer, his own leftovers and putrefactions, by which I mean rough drafts, muddled or shapeless beginnings. When these imperfect efforts contain thoughts that have come from your innermost selves, when they translate the attempt of your whole being to express something right, when they sum up one moment of well-being, they should not be neglected or thrown into the holocaust. It is fitting that you be respectful of the spirit that dwells in you, even if only an apprentice or a diligent child. The Word stammers in all of you.

Not only are you happily influenced by this former self that the patina of time and distance has made to seem something other than you while remaining yours; there is also a pleasure—and an economy—in knowing that nothing you have produced is lost. These fragments can become part of more elaborate combinations. There is not always such a great difference between the labors of your youth and the work of your maturity, between the intuitions of adolescence and the ideas of your seasoned years. The ferments of youth are excessive and awkward; you sense outside influences and the defiance or the imitation of those influences, but everything that is authentic is in the nature of a seed. One must say to the young student: "Don't throw it away. Write. Keep it for yourself. It will help you in papers you have to write later. It will be tested by time, purified by skill, and clothed in the authority that comes simply with the fact of age." Old men and young men do not speak so differently if the young are at all perspicacious; what would be taken as impertinence coming from young lips becomes wisdom when uttered by the old. Throughout literary history you can find examples of the major work of a lifetime that may have taken its first form in a youthful essay. You can find it in Henry James's masterpiece, "The Golden Bowl," where he brings to fruition the development of a technique, the skeleton of which had appeared long before in his first major work, "Roderick Hudson."

Everyone can compose for himself what the Old Testament was for the Jews: a dozen notebooks or portfolios in which are found all the old courses, drafts, work papers, notes, a few poems, some resolutions made and maybe followed, some even more private, almost unsharable hymns—like the Song of Songs. And when such a person has reached, say, thirty-five, he would rule that the book of his youth was closed, that it was inspired, and reading here and there in it of an evening up until the time he was an old man, he himself would find inspiration in it.

# 9

# Writing
# and Style

A great deal of human energy is spent in using words. Herein lies the art of selling, the art of persuading, the art of loving, the art of governing—maybe even the art of self-persuasion. If you admire heroes of the past for their great deeds, you admire no less the art with which they have told of them. You expect your public figures today to be orators as well as leaders.

Even people who profess to despise words concede that they have a power that I, for my part, find often disturbing. The ability to speak well in public was, as late as a century ago, the supreme purpose of education. The path to this art lay via the classical languages; one studied the ancient orators and tried to imitate them.[1] Today, for reasons that are partly good, partly dubious, the art of expression is tending to disappear. People spend less and less time studying it. There is a widespread belief that the essential thing is to *know*, and that

[1] Anyone tempted to disparage this method too quickly should read what Sainte-Beuve wrote about his training in rhetoric and see how, at the age of seventeen, he had already mastered analytical tools that served him all his life. Artificial as the method may be, he achieved this by practicing the art of oratory.

the person who knows will, by extension, be able to speak of what he knows. This is not so. There is an essential connection or interplay between thought and language, and you cannot excel in the one without relying upon the other. Empty, bombastic speech is deplored, and rightly. An old-fashioned rhetoric is unacceptable to our modern sensibilities except in our courts, parliaments, and pulpits. But this much being granted, you discover that you have supplied no valid substitute. Young people are filled with facts and ideas but they are too often incapable of communicating them. The crisis in secondary and higher education comes in part from the fact that intelligent, thoughtful students are so inept in the use of their own language. I am not saying that you need go back to the old-time "eloquence." You must preserve merely its substance, but in new forms that are attuned to the modern mind, a mind more lively and quick, sharper, more candid, more daring, more direct in going to the heart of the matter.

Some people suppose that form is added or tacked on to content, like an ornament. Were this true, concern with form would be an optional, sophisticated preoccupation, and substance alone would be important. Science supplies the content, these people say; the humanities teach form. Ergo, if necessary, one can get along without the humanities. Such opinions bespeak ignorance of what composition means. To compose is to order thought—to search out its various elements, its periods and phases. If it is true that thought can scarcely be distinguished from its inner number and order, then to think is to compose.

On the other hand, whether you are writing or speaking, it is not enough to address yourself to other minds. You must still touch that point where reason is nourished and from which order itself comes. Talking to the "heart" is a difficult operation, and who is to say what the rules of such an art are. Having searched for them, Pascal concluded there were none unless, he said, it be to test one's thought on one's own heart. In his way, Flaubert was giving the same advice when he recommended reading aloud the sentence just written.

To try to compose something is to move toward what is true. To express yourself is to draw near to the beautiful. And once again, you must remember that these two actions are carried out in unison, for beauty is a way of advancing toward truth, just as truth naturally radiates from the beautiful. To compose is to seek balance and proportion—in other words, beauty. In expressing yourselves you are striving to translate through language not merely an intimate truth of a personal, inner order but one corresponding to the truth of all existence. A contemporary French writer said that the more style a work possesses the richer it is in meaning, "the task of style being nothing more than to invest language with meaning." Buffon remarked earlier on the same thing, in words one could easily attribute to Flaubert or Valéry: "All the intellectual felicities that are found in a fine style, all the interconnections of which it is composed, are truths as useful and perhaps even more precious to the public mind than those that may comprise the substance of the matter."

Style, then, is the signature the workman appends to his work. For a book to be human, it must do more than make you think about its subject matter; it must also report discreetly on the thoughts of its author and, allowing you to read between the lines, let you glimpse his face. This applies to scientific works, too, for there is more than one way of presenting the same order of facts. Style is not, then, the same thing as correct lan-

guage; incorrect language is beautiful when it results
not from ignorance but from a revealing motion of the
mind. There is, furthermore, a connection between style
and survival. The classical authors you still read today
are not those who said the truest things but those whose
language has preserved a trace of the "I."

All this bears on the teaching of your native language.
It counsels against the stubborn habit textbook exercises
have of separating content and form, or the overly sharp
distinction drawn between a draft, in which carelessness
is considered permissible, and a finished paper. Literary
work, no matter what its nature, cannot be broken down
into two moments, the first of which would be the
search for truth and the second its translation into correct language. Form and content must arise out of chaos
and indolence via the same effort. Often it happens that
content proceeds from form, or so poets seem to be saying when they speak of their work. And since you have
less power over ideas than over words (because ideas are
few, abstract, and disembodied), you often make the
idea sound forth by pressing on the keyboard of language. This suggests that when a child is still so small
that he does not yet have enough ideas, the greatest
help you can give him is to people his memory with
beautiful forms; for the moment the forms will be void
but later they will summon up for him both meaning
and criteria of usage. The prerequisite for being original
is to know your own language well; that is, to have
mastered its established structures. This is why all classical, formal instruction may often require the student
to learn without understanding, why it is addressed not
to comprehension but to the cadences of memory. Certainly, you must also awaken sensation, develop and
guide initiative, help the student to get the feel of
things, but he would have to be a young genius to sense
that his most profitable exercise is the "learning by

heart" he so dreads. Yet if the son of man does not have one or two languages at his command, he will not rejoice in his world. He will be like a blind man, for he will possess things but he will not possess the Word, which is the light of all things.

How can you teach the man-child language? What kind of exercises can give him sound language training?

A vast amount of advice is to be found in treatises, both old and new, on the art of writing. Clearly, the best of rules in language, as in all matters where art is involved, is to keep in constant contact with models, to frequent the masters—to be impregnated by them, in other words.

## II

When you set about formulating a general principle from which you might derive rules of style, you notice that most of these rules are based on the wish to please.

The first prerequisite for pleasing is to avoid fatigue or ennui. For example, if you criticize a certain way of writing because it is confusing, that is because clarity of expression makes the work of the intelligence easier. If you praise a cadenced, periodic style, it is because cadence, period, and rhythm supply the reader in advance with the mold into which ideas will be cast; they give him a presentiment of things to come that lessens the effort he must make to understand. If, on the other hand, some stylists like Montesquieu or Baudelaire recommend writing in uneven cadences, it is because a too rigid cadence wearies the mind whereas surprise delights it, and surprise is caused by a break in rhythm. The two rules just given, then, although they seem contradictory, are explained by the same law: you must always adapt yourselves to the conditions in which the intelligence of a creature of flesh and blood, whose nervous system is delicate, functions best. The art of style consists in playing on this system like drawing a bow over the strings of a violin. Once again you must remember that mental energy is limited and that each futile effort will take away the strength needed at another point. If style is attuned to these necessities, the euphoria it provides will pass from the reader's eye to his mind and allow him to embrace an idea without being put off by the intermediary of language. If he does linger over the language, it will only be to enjoy the way it harmonizes with the thought, and to be astonished at so improbable, so happy an accident—what is otherwise called a pleasure. How rare it is that between your thoughts—those solitary fruits of the mind—and the words of human speech—so poorly fashioned to bear the fruit—you achieve any consonance!

## III

If style is the inner man made visible, the movement of thought made manifest, it is drawing near to speech. But speech is virtually impossible if you have made in advance a rigid plan of what you want to say. You speak well in response *to* something, when you are spurred by an emotion that unifies you, as when you reply quickly to a friend or opponent.

This is why, once school is behind you and even during that period, it is advisable not to work too hard over how you express yourselves. Speech clothes your thought naturally, except in the case of people who, whether from conventionality or an excessive nicety, force themselves to speak otherwise than they feel. Your chances of writing well are greater if you put yourselves in the frame of mind of the man who improvises under the spur of a lively feeling—irritation, for example. One of your greatest living stylists once confessed to me that in order to write well he had to pretend he was furious. And it is true, a man who is beside himself with anger always has style. So does the man who says little, and that little after a long silence. His remarks are like proverbs. People have reported how in a discussion Pascal used to speak at such a pitch of feeling that everyone invariably thought he was angry. Bonaparte was the same, as was Stendhal, who imitated him in this. I think sometimes of a much earlier man, the evangelist Mark, and imagine him writing "in anger," as he often presents Our Lord to us: *iratus est Jesus.*

These examples should be a lesson for the rest of you who follow more modest paths. You must give up the rules that were so necessary at first—the outline, the draft, and revision. Or rather, you must learn to think of them differently.

No more pre-established outlines that check the mind's forward leap and make the work of the imagination resemble the plodding of a clerk intent on filling up his pigeonholes. It is no longer a question of devising an outline but rather of determining an axis, which is a very different thing. The axis is a plan for life; the plan is the axis of death. When Pascal first spoke of his projected apologia, he had a plan for it in mind. But he came to see that the most perfect scheme must give way under the pressure of a new development that will spring from the free and fertile mind. "I will write my thoughts down as they come," he said then, "but for all that, perhaps not in confusion or without design. No order will be the true order, which will always stamp my purpose by its very disorder."

It takes an effort to discover this second kind of order,

which is quite different from the one I described earlier as useful in composition. It is an effort to gather together and marshal your inner forces and to be honest with yourself, combined with a horror of the banal and the trite. You must take a certain tone. This striving for complete sincerity does not admit of erasures or revisions of what has just been written. In this sense, it is like the *laisser-aller* of the monster; it is a willed, lucid monster drawn from your very entrails.

The question arises: Can these methods be introduced into the classroom? It is sound to learn certain rules about how to write, but this does not give you joy in writing and may even discourage some talented students. I believe that you should have occasional exercises in improvisation. Alain used to train his pupils in this kind of exercise, which requires you to be concise, even abrupt, but always to move on. If one sentence turns out badly, you rescue it in the next. Instead of correcting yourself, you begin afresh, just as you do in life, where you cannot go back over the past and repair it. Goethe held no brief for revising or retouching material. He said to Eckermann, "The thing can become different but not better." This was Péguy's method, too. One of his fellow-students at Sainte-Barbe told me of sitting beside Péguy in class on days when they had composition. When the topic had been announced, he said Péguy would cushion his head on his crossed arms and doze for the first hour, allowing his mind to compose itself around the subject, the way a seed becomes fertile by lying dormant. Then he would rouse himself and in his clear, regal hand write his paper without a falter, like a farmer steadily upturning an even furrow.

Nothing is harder than to begin. I've stopped being surprised that I was never taught about beginnings. The mere idea of getting started with anything is a source of anguish, and then laziness sets in, and finally pride or despair. I think that as far as possible you must avoid having to begin. And the best way to do that is to persevere or to pick up again. The art of finishing, on the other hand, is simple: you interrupt yourself. It would be a good idea to imitate the politician, Pierre Waldeck-Rousseau, who never signaled the end of a speech with any burst of eloquence, so that the band-master used to say, "With the President you never know just when to strike up the Marseillaise."

Stendhal has bequeathed us several trade secrets on this point about beginnings. He discarded the outline or draft methods in favor of inductive passages. He liked to start with a perfectly written fragment. At other times, he used to translate, recopy, or reread a finished page; he might glance over a very old draft manuscript or page from his diary; he might write a description of some painting or engraving. He believed, too, that brevity, the use of interruptions and of jumps contribute to style—ellipsis in all things. The pace should be quickened, he asserted, as the work develops. "Toward the end of a book one should suppress the 'so to speaks' and their ilk. . . . My mind is a lazy thing, and it asks nothing better than to twine itself around anything less difficult than writing." Stendhal eschewed cogitating and agonizing over his work whenever he possibly could. "Stendhal's big secret," Gide tells us, "his great trick is to sit down and start writing at once. . . . What results is something quick, spontaneous, discordant, unexpected. . . . When one hesitates, one is lost."

A few more words of advice. Style must be concealed. This is the old law of purification by pruning. To create is to renounce infinite possibilities in order to retain only one. Yet, like nature, the artist leaves each of his finite creations surrounded by a nimbus of the infinite: in painting this may be achieved by a halo or a tone or shading or by an intentional non-resolution of design; in poetry, by pure and indefinite words; in speech, by glances and silences; in prose, by allusion, by the forms of the conditional, and by an easing of the affirmative statement—the effect contributed by "no doubt," "rather," "perhaps," "in one sense," and so on. The Greeks had a number of such little words for conveying nuance and attenuation. They are hardly to be found in other languages, or at least not in so light and unaccented a form. They add greatly to the perfection of Greek as a language for the expression of ideas.

## IV

Style embraces the art of editing. To edit you must know how to expand and dilute ideas, how to fill up space, how to cover blank paper with significant signs. Even a brief exposure to a language or composition class shows that young people who might manage an aphoristic style are absolutely incapable of editing their own papers; they could imitate Caesar, not Cicero. If such students find composition a bore, it is not that they lack ideas but that they simply do not command the vocabulary and facility in the use of language that they need to develop an idea.

I have thought more than once that a sharper distinction should be drawn between the art of writing and the art of editing. Voltaire rightly observed that "it is easier to sketch brief portraits of things that strike your attention than to write a long imaginative work that at once pleases and instructs you."

In painting there are moments where the one question is a matter of filling space—for example, if you are painting a sky, or a straight fall of cloth, or a shadow.

The same thing occurs in writing a novel or a philosophic work; many pages are there only to compose the mind or to prepare it for what is to come. The first exercise I should like to propose to receptive students is to teach them how to *cover,* by which I mean how to edit the commonplaces. In human intercourse, good manners prescribe our being able to carry on a conversation without asking personal questions or making personal revelations. Yet the painter's sky must be a fine sky; the empty, annunciatory pages of the book must be pages that we read with interest; the unaccented conversation must be sincere. Herein lies a part of the art of talking, writing, and painting. The religious office is admirable in this respect—the psalmody sustains the faltering prayer. It's a good idea to look for the equivalent in the other offices of life. I would say to these young people: "To write pages that must simply fill in space, let your pen run on pretty much where and how it likes, but avoid anything that would be vulgar, and try to remain essentially sincere." To the painter I would say: "Cover this space with colors that are not dull." And to the man of the world: "Say what you like, so long as you are forbearing."

If I had to advise a young writer, I would want to suggest that he first practice connecting, passing from one thing to the next, relating, allowing himself to be borne along by the motion of his pen. In this he would be imitating the motion of life, which does not abound in crises or peaks and is never more itself than when it is simply moving on, tying everything to everything else —continuing, in a word. You should write the way you dash off a letter or the way you talk. Let one word call forth another.

These happy or unhappy associations that now weave together, now unravel, stimulate the mind to choose from among all the fortuities those that have value.

"Thoughts" come to you without your having to "think" of them. Your attention should not be riveted on ideas, you should not strive to be original but simply to link one sentence to another, to hear the words echoing one against the other as you unobtrusively observe them play and copulate.

A good writer should be at once ordinary and extraordinary, monotonous and full of surprises, harmonious yet sometimes abrupt. That is to say, he should be able to imitate nature in presenting us with two aspects, appearing at one moment simple, solid, and firm, yet at the next turn of the road producing something startling. Every writer should keep at his disposal a small private vocabulary, words that he finds matchless and prefers above all others, that become, in a way, his mark or signature and establish a kinship among his modes of expression. What a relief it would be for our students if we allowed them to repeat themselves! "Caesar was persuaded," the Chevalier de Mere said, "that beauty of language depends much more on using the best words than in using a variety of words, and when he found a way of expressing himself that pleased him, he never grew tired of it nor did he fear it would tire others."[2]

Some people are of the opinion that the less intelligibly one writes, the better one has written; that one must use terms understandable only to the initiate. Now, it is true, obscure language can produce an almost religious effect. Also, it demands that you make an effort to understand and, as everyone knows, effort pays off. Yet nothing guarantees that an obscure passage is, by exten-

[2] In an old copy of a magazine I came across the replies of several authors who had been asked to name the ten words they found most beautiful. Maurois had said: Silence, order, beauty, melancholy, charm, smile, tender, fragile, honest, friendly. François Mauriac had answered: Childhood, sleep, dawn, blood, torpor, storm, annunciation, ashes, dust, joy. Paul Valéry: Pure, day, gold, lake, peak, alone, wave, leaf, damp, flute.

sion, a profound passage. I once knew a professor of philosophy who was preparing notes for a quite simple introductory course. He salted and peppered them with what he called "the necessary obscurity," without which, he believed, his wares would not have caught and held the attention of his more adult students. There's a great deal to be said for this. Yet I suspect that obscurity is not the ultimate garb—the last veil, as it were—but the first and definitive state. One is born and one dies obscure. Let anyone who has received from the gods this gift of confusion of thought be consoled and, taking his chances, play the game to the hilt. He risks becoming a prophet, or winning fame and disciples and a church. The obscurity that you agonize over in secret as a kind of impotence is, lo and behold, what some men worship, and there you are, forced to become the priest of a religion that has its roots in your infirmity.

But the technique of obscurity is not learned in school. So far, at least, the school has had to teach you to express everything that is latent or concealed. The teacher's perennial question to a student is "What do you mean?" In the West, the teacher's objective is to prepare the ground for a dialogue between men. Conversation presupposes that you are always able to understand what the other person has said to you. But were you to listen to two mystics conversing, you would notice that each waits silently for the other to finish before beginning his own song.

A useful bit of advice for beginners is to say to them: "In the beginning, write in the first person. You'll come closer to a style if you say 'I' than if you say 'one.'" Some authors actually write their novels as if they were huge, extended confidences and then transcribe them into the impersonal third person. This is probably because that little word 'I' (such a hateful word, according to Pascal, who nonetheless used to say 'I hate')

forces you to become involved. Inspiration being otherwise equal, you have more style when you contradict
than when you affirm, more when you are irritated than
when you remain calm, more when you lament than
when you smile, more when you are describing the dark
places. You are clearer when you dissent, witness the
great Church Councils."


## V


I wrote to a student who had asked help in solving
this impossible problem of language:
"A person should write the way he would talk, if he
talked well. This implies two contradictory practices.
You are to suppose that you are faced with an ignorant
but intelligent student, and you talk with him, you give
him the benefit of your own thoughts the way you
would show him around a garden or through a museum.
This was Fénélon's way, which explains the clarity of
his style; he spoke and wrote as if he were addressing
some young pupil. And Descartes, who is a good writer
thanks to his way of establishing relationships between
ideas, is an even better one when he is writing to the
young refugee princess Elizabeth. The same is true of
Renan, the French historian, writing to his sister Hen-
riette. Montaigne began the Essays in the form of letters
to Mme. d'Estissac; St. Francis de Sales composed his
"Vie Dévote" by putting together letters he had written
to Mme. de Charmoisy. Thought is a confession. And
style is not achieved without the effort to draw out the
thing that dares not show itself. Even in an examination, you must make an effort to relate what you say
with the topic to be considered—to find the joint where
the general question put to you becomes *your* question.
This happens almost without effort in an exchange of

confidences. Which is why the ideal rule would be for
you to address yourselves—like Seneca and St. Jerome
(and Plotinus, too, perhaps?)—to a woman.

"This rule may have a too softening effect, and to
compensate for that I would advise you to maintain a
certain standard of correctness in your conversations
with friends and even when you talk to yourself. It is
never entirely harmless to lapse into vague or exaggerat-
ed statement. It would be much better to use slang,
which is, after all, a poetic language. Never, for example, say 'nice.' It is salutary to make a slight effort and
without being pedantic, to find the least unsuitable
word. Without seeming to, look for a kind of distinction
in even your daily speech. This is the same thing as saying: take the trouble to choose, to be selective.

"Thus, in writing the way you speak and in speaking
a little bit in the way you would like to write, you will
more or less strike a balance, and when the day comes
when you will have to write or speak publicly, you will
have fewer problems of self-expression to struggle over.

"You ask whether one should correct oneself, and how
to set about that. In the field of ethics that would be an
unanswerable question! As for language, I think that
when we have finished a passage, we should cut anything that ignores the rules and anything that respects
them to excess. Carelessness and undue nicety are two
temptations that prevent us from being natural.

"To correct either our behavior or our writing, I
think we must put some distance between ourselves and
the thing in question. It's a good idea to wait until
whatever has come from our innermost selves has become strange and remote. We should do as the mid-
wives do who let the infant alone and take care of the
mother. Taking care of the mother means to be calm,
to replenish ourselves, to accept inevitable mediocrities.
What does it matter that the child is not completely

perfect? He's there, and he's crying lustily. Life is more than nourishment, and the body is more than its garments.

"As to the philosophical style you ask about: it requires an extra effort of coherence and precision. You may say 'and more exactly' or 'it remains to be seen whether' or 'that is to say.' And you may show the joinings, as Julien Benda recommends—'for,' 'in consequence of which,' 'this is why.' But philosophy must have its mystery, too, which a philosophic style introduces via doubt, loftiness, imagery, and sometimes by a completely abstract modulation such as you find in Plato, St. Thomas, and Malebranche. But our taste today is for the aphorism—or the mass effect."

# 10

# Working While
# Tired or Sick

To this point, I have talked about working while one is well. Ours is a time of anxiety and weariness, however, and people rarely find themselves in an optimum working situation. More often, the mid-twentieth-century man must cast about him to find how despite obstacles he can still carry on with his job.

Of all workers, the intellectual worker has least need of health or rest or favorable working conditions. It is hard to imagine what Rembrandt would have achieved had he been deprived of canvas, or a Beethoven without musical instruments. But for a long time Descartes was shut up in a smoky room without books; Pascal did his best work when he was an invalid and had to scribble on any paper he had at hand. And think of Marcel Proust, asthmatic and dying, who could write well only when, bedridden, he lay half-suffocating in a room hazy with inhalations, his bedclothes serving as his desk. You may well wonder about Proust and Pascal: Would health have helped them as much as illness did? The need to make every moment count, the anguish of being perhaps unable to finish, the having to break off, the

forgetting, suffering, sudden flashes of insight—all these
accompaniments to a physical ailment stimulated their
minds. Epicurus was an invalid, too, and sat in a rose-
laurel garden, only rising now and then to note down
some thought. Lucretius was undoubtedly even more
seriously ill. St. Paul wrote, ". . . we are being hampered
everywhere, yet still have room to breathe, are hard put
to it, but never at a loss. . . ." (II Cor., 4:8). Nietzsche,
reflecting on the root of life, wondered about the nature
of illness, and came to see in it a means to self-realiza-
tion.

Must a person give up working when he is tired or in
pain—for example, in the lapses caused by a minor illness? Obviously, severe illness or total destitution makes
it impossible to concentrate. But the trials of life have
their rhythms and moments of surcease when you can
find place for nonphysical work, although it may not be
termed intellectual effort.

## II

Our textbooks, preachers, and moralists correctly describe will as a power that, having once decided on
something, mobilizes itself for action, rejects conflicting
ideas, and perseveres in this dual course of concentration on one thing and rejection of all else. But to this
action of consciousness upon consciousness is juxtaposed,
and sometimes substituted, an action of the conscious
mind upon the unconscious or of the unconscious upon
the conscious, which is a very different thing. This is an
effort which is really non-effort. The problem here is to
avoid an inversion that is almost always fatal to any
sustained application of the mind.

A time comes when the effort applied against an external obstacle quickens an inner, more insidious ob-

stacle, which is magnified in proportion to your denying it. You can see this in the stutterer. Moral philosophers who have studied the mechanism of temptation are aware of it. To be tempted is to find yourself at grips with an image you know is going presently to act upon the glands. Attempts to direct your energies so as to dissipate the image are likely only to intensify it. The body does not know the difference between "yes" and "no." To say "I am not afraid, I am not afraid, I am not afraid of this shell that is screaming overhead" is to strengthen the terrifying images that beset you. Trying not to shake during an examination makes you shake all the more. Becoming rigid because you want not to fall into temptation puts you in a condition where you are more likely to give in. Very likely this is why you are advised to pray that you not be tempted rather than that you be helped to resist, for the latter is so very hard.

This law of inversion that governs poorly directed effort is one of the most profound laws of our psychic life. I am amazed that so little is said or taught about it. When I have been unable to learn a simple skill—geometry or horseback riding, for example—despite excellent guidance and good will on my own part, it has been because my teachers did not know this law of inversion. I would stiffen over the horse's rump or over the theorem, and all I got was a fall or a total blank. You must work feeling relaxed. "Laugh!" the Duke de Nemours used to say to his sons when he saw them stumble in the manège. "Laugh!" Joan of Arc gave the same advice to the Bastard.

Bergson used to say to friends that there were two ways of mounting a horse. One was the army sergeant's technique: anxiety, tension, keeping at it, albeit bruised and bloody—in a word, sweating it through. In general, this is not such a bad system and I think it works for most people. The other way is to be attuned to the motions of the animal, being as supple and responsive as possible, careful not to break the gait of this agile creature, and giving yourself over, as Bergson put it, to "the grace of horsemanship," as if it were a gift that had been given you. Very likely the first method will see you through from one day to the next, as you can see in people learning to dance or to speak a foreign language. One thing is sure: to learn to act effortlessly (whatever the action; it may even be attaining to virtue), you have to make a great many preliminary tries.

I would not dare recommend the non-effort method to teachers of very young children. But for the adolescent or mature man, or for the artist, or for the invalid, there is none better. This is all the more true, since the effort to make no effort is extraordinarily difficult—the way, in comparison to other virtues, renunciation is hard.

The art of non-effort consists in never letting your will become aroused or tensed. Imitate nature's wild creatures; let go, in a way, in order to "tame the will," as Montaigne said, by which he meant wanting something wittingly *and* at the right moment, always mindful of the fact that the will, being a vital energy, also grows tired and falters.

There is a state of rather relaxed, slightly absent thought which assists memory, invention and writing. It is probably what Descartes used to call "admiration," which he ranked above love as being its precondition and first realization. Effort is praiseworthy, of course, but according to a very profound Christian idea, it is useful and salutary only if it is deployed in the far-seeing, supportive, and consummating state called a state of grace, which is the very opposite of effort. Through grace the melody of measure prevails in you; grace allows you to evade the promptings of the will, and fixed ideas and obsessions. Without grace, effort is futile and even exacerbates the state that previously prevailed. What would your awareness of sin be without grace? It would make your heads turn and hurl you into the very thing you dread. Whatever the undertaking may be, the most propitious attitude with which to approach it is the one that imitates or resembles grace. Maeterlinck said that Novalis "smiled at things with gentle indifference; he looked on the world with the attentive curiosity of an idle angel." This is the kind of attention Raphael recommended; he said that when a man is painting he must not think about anything, in which case "everything does then present itself better." The design may be somewhat discontinuous in such circumstances, but the artist avoids the kind of effort that is detrimental and he is freer to be himself. Daydreaming, letting your pen run on. . . . Everything comes from this. The secret of creating is, in many cases, to dream and then to order the dream.

## III

If this is true, then it is possible to study when you are tired or ill. Fatigue does not inhibit sustained thought, and all you need is a pencil and note pad by your chair to sketch out the dream or idea, not bothering unduly about form but being rather relaxed, which will coax your ideas forth. Anxiety can be utilized, too; you have only to write on casually to see it gradually dissipate and disappear.

Copying is an even easier operation, and can be very welcome if you are feeling at low ebb. You cannot copy without becoming a part of the thing copied; and there is a particularly restful way of copying, which consists in writing in a large hand, not bothering with a carbon, but writing an occasional note in the margins, changing a few expressions here and there—playing, casually, with the text. Such copies are worthwhile because you discover that you have easily become a part of them, you avoid the stumbling block of having to choose a topic, then getting started, finding the right word, and so on. Your thoughts are drawn into a dream, portions of which stay with you, and you can feel confident that they are truly good and helpful. Great artists are not afraid to follow this procedure; for example, in the copy Rembrandt made of Leonardo's "Last Supper," the grouping of the apostles remains the same, but their movements are simplified and softened. Rembrandt brings the groups to the right and left of Christ nearer to Him; he substitutes assymetrical outlines for the horizontal balancing of the farther groups. It is Leonardo's disposition of forms, but with fresh movements that are more human and baroque.

It would be possible, I think, to carry these methods of free reproduction further. But you would promptly suppose it to your discredit to acknowledge that you depend on or borrow from others. A part of art consists in concealing such underpinnings. In school we push students to write on their own too early, as if they were all Aristotles or Descartes—neither of whom, for that matter, was afraid to borrow ideas from other men. Today who would dare assign as an important paper the imitation or paraphrasing or rewriting of some distinguished work the student has read? I used to watch a scholarly colleague when he was working on his translation of the Aeneid. He sat with three published translations open in front of him, and once he had read and chewed over the Latin original, he would take a look at what his predecessors had done: "What did Delille say here?" "How did Charpentier put that?" Often he used to upbraid them for not capturing the Vergilian tone, which, without their help, he might not have discovered

himself. Gide said wisely, "A great man has only one
concern—to become as human as possible; or, let's put
it better, *to become banal.* . . . The remarkable thing
is, he in this way becomes more himself. Whereas the
man who acts out his humanity as if it were a role only
manages to become peculiar, bizarre, defective. . . .
Might I quote the Gospel? Yes, for I don't believe I am
distorting the sense of it: 'Whosoever shall seek to save
his life shall lose it; and whosoever shall lose his life
shall preserve it' (Luke, 17:33). Or, to translate the
Greek more faithfully, 'he will make it more truly alive.'
For this reason, as we can see, lofty minds never fear
influences but, on the contrary, seek them out with an
avidity that is like the avidity to *be*."

Illness, fatigue, moments in which you feel empty or
absent—and all of you know such times—make it easier
for you to achieve this state of docile vacancy, when you
can look about for a helpful influence—that is, for a
current flowing in the direction of your own that therefore strengthens it. When you write a book, what do you
hope for if not that some mind be sufficiently unoccu-
pied really to read what you have written and to let
itself be silently invaded? Periods of mild sickness, fast-
ing, imprisonment, or convalescence are particularly
conducive to this. Time spent in a prisoner-of-war camp
or a sanatorium has allowed many of our contemporaries to recapture the leisure so beloved of the Greeks
that is not truly productive unless it is accompanied by
pain.

Here is the advice a doctor gave to some convalescent
tuberculosis patients: "Please don't just kill the time
you've got—it's all the more precious for being short—
by playing cards or listening to some radio slop or leafing
through picture magazines. Those of you who want to,
will find a way of using this time—in work which, since
it cannot be physical work, will be work with your hands

or heads. The returns on the hours you spend persevering at some task or other are sometimes surprising; slight as the job may be, your taste for work and your pleasure in it will be kept alive; your work potential will not have run down by the time you are discharged. Also, the habit of exerting yourself to do something will be an indispensable support for your morale."

People who are seriously ill obviously cannot manage to carry on sustained work. Their work is subject to constant interruption. That is why Nietzsche, like Pascal, wrote only in lightning-like flashes. But these fragments that spring from suffering instruct you all the more.

## IV

We all know more than one author who despite frail health has left his mark no less decisively than others perfectly sound in constitution, for the true strength is the strength of the spirit. In teaching, abundance is a virtue, witness the Church Fathers whose "conversations," in the sense of *sermo,* posterity has preserved. But illness has dedicated others to brevity. I want to quote from one of this breed of men—a man who spent his youth working so intensively that he was an invalid for the rest of his life. This is the advice Henri de Tourville gave friends when they complained of being unable to accomplish enough (I am quoting from several letters) :

"I've been confined to my room since December 27th, down with anemia and grippe again, and virtually unable to work. . . . Do your work in a hit-or-miss fashion. Take time off to recoup your energy; be sluggish; send your mind off on vacation, as it were. Meanwhile, collect the ideas and insights that will still come to you now and then; do this, and you will have done something that will stand you in good stead later on. See to it that you have a few unstrenuous, beguiling projects that you can pick up and set aside at will. Take from them what appeals to you and leave the rest; presently you will discover that you have actually moved ahead and have gleaned a not too poor harvest. . . . What I am recommending is some agreeable work or study that you can readily take up or put down, which occupies your mind without overstraining it—indeed, quite the contrary, it will tend to keep the mind fit by feeding it something of interest when it is thoroughly tired. To find such an activity, all you need to do is not look too hard for it, which would spoil all the charm. For that matter, you should have more than one such interest— three or four would not be too many, but one would be too few. The diversity is immensely helpful; we must not feel nailed down to a single chore. . . .

"Prepare your work while also preparing the tool you have for it—which is utter frankness, an entirely new disposition of your faculties that are now relaxed and rested and receptive. Do not fret that circumstances allow you to do only so much, that at this rate it will take you ten years, and so on and so on. Love your new chore for itself. Let it be potent and restoring and satisfying for you in and of itself. Let yourself enjoy it without feeling too vexed that you cannot make everyone else enjoy it as much as you would like. One step leads to another. Who can help but feel the stimulus a man exudes who in his inner life is so very much alive that he seems to carry within him a whole world in which he expands and flourishes?"

You never know when or where or in what form a word, a thought, a book will open up and flower. Believers lay great stress on our smallest actions' having delayed or disproportionate effects. They see such actions as the roots of a bush that will grow only in the afterlife. There is a lot of sense in this, even for the person who cannot relate it to the idea of eternity, and who must be satisfied with that image of eternity which is the mystery of the future. You do not know when or how the pollen which is the present will germinate, what will be the offspring of the word you now pronounce, of the thing you now do. I was watching a friend of mine while he filed away the most insignificant odds and ends of correspondence and when I reproached him for it, he retorted, "Who knows? How can you know what is significant and what is not? Here is an invitation to a funeral. Five hundred years from now, this card which I refuse to throw away will help some historian reconstruct our customs. What wouldn't we give to have just such 'insignificant' documents from the Romans or the Egyptians?"

You need ideas like this to bolster your confidence when you feel lost. Provided you are present in spirit or wish, nothing is ever devoid of meaning; everything can admit of post-factum significance. Actually, it is worth noting that immediate success is a bad sign; a work that receives immediate recognition risks exhausting in the furtive present its potentiality for having manifold meanings. The posthumous work carries more weight, for it has greater value, surrounded as it is by the dead presence of the author who, one may suppose, is reading, too, and thereby assisting your thoughts. Furthermore, the posthumous work is not tarnished by the author's desire to reap the pleasures of being admired and recognized. If you did not have personal responsibilities to others, if you could do without the whip of criticism and praise, if you were sure enough that not only do you belong to your own time but are also translating the eternity of man, then you should try to reserve your work for the honor of posthumous publication and

entrust it meanwhile to your executor. For the end
alone gives meaning to the beginning, the last writings
throw light on the first, and the final acts of a life il-
lumine the whole. A person's last thoughts—as you can
see in the example of St.-Exupéry or Simone Weil—
have the authority of sacraments and final testaments.


## V

Nevertheless, whatever the mental work you are engaged in may be, you do encounter moments of depres-
sion and anguish.

During your school years, this misery is largely external to the work itself. It comes from your being forced
to perform out of fear or youthful jealousy or apprehen-
sion about passing and graduating. The pleasures of
those years are also for the most part external—winning
a prize, being given a reward, basking in a parent's
smile or in general approval. It is possible to grow in
knowledge and even to win repeated success in school
without loving study but only the laurels that the system
has devised as incentives.

The further you advance, the more intimate the labor
pains become. For that matter, this is the law of pro-
longed suffering: as it continues and develops, everything becomes interiorized. The idea of competition per-
sists in an obscure and most insidious way, which is
competition with yourself—despair at not being equal to
your best. To this you must add the hardships of solitary
intellectual life: its monotony; its knots; the fluctuations
of mood; the experience of seeing the exact truth or its
exact expression so rarely achieved; the dismay at seeing
false virtues triumph and true ones pass unrecognized;
the difficulty of maintaining mastery over your own
mind; even the choices you must make, which are less

and less often imposed by others or by circumstances but which you must find in yourselves. I add here the feeling in Ecclesiastes and in "The Imitation" of the vanity of all that is written (beyond the area of evidence), of the mounting precariousness of the world into which you send your message forth, and of that law decreeing that most of the sowing shall be lost and only the most unlikely seed germinate.

A source of uneasiness that is peculiar to intellectual work comes from the fact that you do not possess innate standards by which to judge it. The wheel of the wheelbarrow, if it is well made, satisfies you and proves itself by rolling smoothly; the electronic microscope reassures the man who devised the wave-transmission theory. But an essay on nothingness, or a fine poem—how are they to be tested? What is to tell you whether they will be remembered ten years hence? It is lucky that the public is not allowed to eavesdrop while a jury of experts judges the too original or the very mediocre entry. Or that the candidate for a degree cannot see the pen of his examiner hover coolly between a passing and failing mark, while his whole future hangs in the balance; he would insist on the powers-that-be granting him a review and still another; he would demand that a statistical evaluation be substituted for personal judgment— and he would be wrong. It is unwise to want to escape the uncertainties of the human condition, to avoid the risk that is present in all things. Better to have seen how the land lies and to accept what comes.

The most wonderful part of intellectual work—even at the secondary-school level, where it is so encumbered with conventions—is that the work is a mirror and prelude of what will be lavished on you later in life. The child who does his utmost and who loses heart, the one who tries so hard and long and finally fails, the fellow whose teacher doesn't understand him or who doesn't understand his teacher—all of them are learning far more about life than about grammar or mathematics. In the same way and to an even greater degree, this holds true for the solitary student who does not have the support of assigned work and must discipline himself. You rarely hear teachers emphasize this resemblance between school and life, yet to my mind this is the chief secret of all instruction: What would be the point of studying if it did not preadapt you to rules that are so full of exceptions, to pleasures that are so shadowed by troubles, to all the chances that will loom tomorrow like enigmatic constellations by which you will have to chart your course? The subject matter you study is often useless: What is the point, the student asks himself, of my writing this Latin theme? I'm never going to speak Latin. This line of reasoning could be applied to almost all our daily occupations. You can surmount it only by assigning an absolute value to the act of attention, to formal excellence, and to this day's effort. By which I mean, you must believe that your act of attention, your holding firm, your effort to achieve perfection even in minutiae, offer their own reward and justification, quite aside from any practical result or profit that may accrue from them. The poet will understand what I am saying here.

Her life provides full authority for what Simone Weil has to say:

"If one really concentrates on finding the solution to a problem in geometry, and if after an hour one is no nearer an answer than when one started, one has nonetheless moved forward every minute of that hour into another and more mysterious domain. Without your feeling it, without your knowing it, this seemingly sterile and fruitless effort has drawn more light into your spirit. Sometime later the fruit will be found again in prayer. It will no doubt be found also, by extension, in some province of the intelligence that may be utterly alien to mathematics. . . . An Eskimo folk tale explains the origin of light in this way: 'The crow, who could not, in the eternal night, find food, wished for light, and the earth became light.' If there really is desire, and if the desire is really for light, the desire for light will produce light. . . . The futile efforts of the Curé d'Ars to learn Latin over those long, painful years bore their entire fruit in his marvelous ability to discern the very souls of his confessants behind their words and even behind their silences."

And so it is that intellectual effort, in its entirety as in its parts, from the a-b-c of infancy to old age, teaches you that the balance to be carried forward is related to time as you can know it in this world, and that the moment of sowing is not the same as the moment of reaping.

Where you have sown, however, you must encourage the seed to germinate and flower. "Where" means a given moment or a given place, this day or that, these surroundings, such and such limits. If you will have done no more than to correct one of your own sentences to be less inexact, if you will have done no more than to say one word that may induce another person to think better and therefore to do better, if you will have done no more than to increase your knowledge by one small particle, this will be enough, if on each of these fragments you have placed the stamp of your spirit.

"Given that"—this familiar phrase from geometry is also applicable to the problem of man and his use of time; that which is given you at this moment, you shall accept, improve, and enlarge. Then you will be truly alive.

# 11

# Excerpts from
# a Letter
# to a Young Man

Before you close this little book, young man—whatever your race or your country or your faith—let me say one or two things more.

If the preceding chapters have any purpose at all, it is, as I said, to reassure you. You do not have much self-confidence. And you are wrong. You will be able to do what you want if you want it with art and with perseverance. At your age, the mere words "ten years" are terrifying. I tell you that ten years are very little. Look at what you have learned from your tenth to your fifteenth year; add to that what you could still learn if you wanted to, or if you were forced to, as a young boy is forced to learn in school.

Perfection is not so far away from you. You can lose an awful lot of time looking for the best book, the best method, the best friend! The old teacher who was asked by a student which was the best textbook on his subject, answered, "My friend, the one you've got in your hand." You might add that the best moment is this moment; the best group of friends, the ones you have; the best thought, the one that comes to mind now.

So don't go looking for the best. Instead, invest what you have in hand now, what you are doing at present, with the dignity of being best.

Do not, indeed, put off until tomorrow what you can do today, but at the same time never fail to put off until tomorrow everything that does not fit into the so narrow capacity of the present. In other words, fill the passing moment with some thing, no matter how little, and postpone ambition until infinity.

Accept your limitations on every side. Limits give form, and form is a condition of plenitude.

No doubt you are going to have to pass through the gristmill of college and perhaps, depending on where you have been born, through competitive examinations. This is an essential part of the game to which you must lend yourself, but be mindful to keep yourself for you.

The important thing is to remain above your work— by which I mean that you must make your work serve you, make it contribute to your sound growth. To that end, I think there is only one useful piece of advice to give you, misunderstood or travestied as it has always been and always will be: "Look for the truth. Say only what you believe you know, and keep quiet about the rest. Express yourself sincerely and directly, and avoid all bombast. Go to the heart of things, to their pure and authentic essence. If it happens that you, having discovered the truth, will have to communicate it to others, do so in the way that is closest to your inner truth."

Cherish all that is genuine, and because of this love be on your guard not to associate exclusively with intelligent people. Do not voluntarily frequent the person who is like you; you will meet him often enough in life.

So often what we call intelligence today is a kind of sensitizing of the mind to what is too fine, too subtle to be grasped by the ordinary tools of knowledge; it is the abstract idea, the ideal divorced from practical application, or yet again paradox or nuance. This exercise is hard; it is exhausting. It requires your making your mind as palpitatingly responsive as a delicate membrane, greedy for the absolute, the unusual, and the rarified; easily offended, ungrateful, caring passionately for only a few things. The intellectual temperament, after all, is hypersensitive, although it is believed to be cold and impartial. You will notice, however, that intellectuals cannot accept criticism in good part, for all that they themselves are fond of criticizing. This is true of even the most calm and constructive ones, men like Descartes and Pasteur. The intelligent man tends as a means of self-preservation to live with admirers. You should be able to overhear intellectuals saying things like "I was wrong." . . . "You were right." . . . "I must think that over." But you will notice how rarely you hear anything of the sort in conversations between intellectuals.

Another source of grief. Your intelligence should help you to adapt to everything, since what is intelligence if not the capacity to become all things. Yet it must be admitted that intelligence often cuts us off or makes us rigid. The horror some people feel at the thought of their being taken for pedants can drive them into an inverse pedantry. For example, I have known some widely cultivated people who are studiously profane; dogmatic people who hide their stubborn convictions behind a perpetual smile; men who hunger for absolute truth and who cannot speak without irony, pretending to believe in nothing.

Also, I have asked myself—and here I am speaking of what I have seen in France—why is it that generally our great writers do not come from among the ranks of fellowship students or the graduates of our fine arts universities; why art and science, not to speak of religion, have so often been enriched and renewed by minds that are either relatively untrained or that have been active in specialized lines of work quite different from those in which they later excel. The explanation cannot be that the people who are preparing for advanced academic work are less good material. I have taught classes in which the students were preparing for postgraduate work in the humanities and in the sciences, and I know from experience that you find among them the best of French youth, from the point of view both of native intelligence and unflagging energy. Why, then, do you see them with the passing of time often become stiff and turn into automatons or imitations of their former selves, as if they were preparing for competitive exams their whole life long? Are we in France not placing too heavy a burden on young minds? Is it right to define the value of a man in terms of the skill, quickness, and good luck that are his at eighteen? Observing such things, I am moved to denounce the French system that seizes on our finest young people, promises them the earth, and proceeds to work them to death; that cuts them off, more often than not, from the joy of creating new forms or even the pleasure of putting to good use those that have been discovered by others. The British method seems to elicit more from human nature; it allows for more leisure; it does not force young people to strive so hard to emulate others except in the harmless area of sports; it postpones specialization to a more mature age. The result is that in the Englishman's median and productive years, his face is not haggard with the lines of his youth, for his youth sustains and energizes him.

The ideal would be to have a teacher who is skillful at simplification initiate you rather early into everything

that is really indispensable to your specialized field,
whatever it may be, so that you avoid the futile awk-
wardnesses of beginning. Then you should be given
relatively free time and be allowed to follow your own
impulses. This is precisely the favor that the older de
Broglie was able to do for his younger brother Louis.
Louis took his degree in history, specializing in the
Middle Ages, and then abruptly turned to mathematics
and took up the study of quanta; in this way, he escaped the scholastic preparation that repels and shackles
a young mind. In another order of work, it was the
same for Cézanne; they taught him merely how to handle a canvas, colors, and brushes—and I suspect that an
hour was enough. The rest he gave himself, face to face
with nature in his beloved Provence, which was his only
teacher.

The important thing is to do what the venerable author of Ecclesiastes advised: "Wherefore I perceive
that there is nothing better, than that a man should rejoice in his own works; for that is his portion."